D0372828

Michele Wates graduated f
with a first class honours deg
Education. She currently lives   with her partner
and two children. Her experience of parenting has taken
place in the context of a slowly progressive condition
(MS), and an equally slow, but liberating, progress towards
setting up a wheelchair accessible lifestyle. Michele Wates
has been involved over a number of years in a
campaigning and support network of disabled parents,
and is the author of one previous book, based on her
research in that area.

The power of a story, well told, is something she has
been aware of throughout her life and that is one of the
reasons why she is delighted to have been involved in
this anthology.

Rowen Jade is a survivor of mainstream education. She
graduated from Oxford Brookes University with a first
class honours degree in English Literature and Law, began
working with The Alliance for Inclusive Education and
now works as a Disability Equality Trainer. She is
currently the Director of Different Perspectives, a training
and consultancy company. Rowen strongly believes that
disabled people will only be free when every disabled
person has control of their own life.

Having been a wheelchair user throughout childhood,
Rowen stopped sitting up at the age of 14; she came out
as a lesbian aged 24; and, with her Australian partner, is
now making plans to become a parent. Rowen has always
travelled beyond the limitations of conformity and her
hope is that, one day, difference will truly be celebrated.

UCD WOMEN'S CENTRE/DU

For disabled women of all time and everywhere

bigger than the sky

Disabled Women on Parenting

Michele Wates and Rowen Jade, editors

First published by The Women's Press Ltd, 1999
A member of the Namara Group
34 Great Sutton Street, London EC1V 0LQ

Collection copyright © Michele Wates and Rowen Jade 1999

The copyright in each of the pieces in this collection remains with
the original copyright holder.

The right of the contributors to be identified as the joint authors of
this work has been asserted by them in accordance with the
Copyright, Designs and Patents Act 1988.

The following pieces are adaptations of previously published material,
reprinted by kind permission:
Rosangela Berman Bieler, 'The Rights to Maternity', from *One in Ten*, a
publication on childhood disability edited by UNICEF and Rehabilitation
International, Spring 1998.
Sylvia Dick Gomez, 'Reflections of a Mama Bear', *Felkdenkrais Journal*, No 11,
Winter 1996.
Chava Willig Levy, 'Tehilah: Our Answered Prayer', winner of the EDI Media
Award for portraying disability with dignity, originally appeared in *McCall's*
magazine, December 1991.
Micheline Mason, 'Reclamation', from *New Internationalist*, No 300, April 1998,
pp12–14.
Denise Sherer Jacobson, 'The Seeds of Trust' in her book *The Question of David*,
Creative Arts Book Company, Berkeley, 1999.
Michele Wates, 'Are You Sure You Can Cope?', from *Disabled Parents: Dispelling
the Myths*, The Radcliffe Medical Press and NCT publishing, 1997.
The editors wish to thank Jo Somerset and Ben for permission to use Sue
Napolitano's poem, 'Child'.

British Library Cataloguing-in-Publication Data
A catalogue record for this book is available from the British Library.

This book is sold subject to the condition that it shall not, by way of
trade or otherwise, be lent, re-sold, hired out, or otherwise circulated
without the Publisher's prior consent in any form of binding or
cover other than that in which it is published and without a similar
condition including this condition being imposed on the
subsequent purchaser.

ISBN 0 7043 4545 5

Typeset in Stone Serif by FSH Ltd, London
Printed and bound in Great Britain by Cox & Wyman Ltd,
Reading, Berkshire

Contents

Introduction

As soon as we read Adina Frieden's autobiographical essay, 'Bigger than the Sky', we realised that we had been sent far more than a moving piece of writing; we had been given a title for the whole anthology. From the outset, our aim in compiling this anthology was to examine the links between disability and parenting from many different points of view. We wanted to expose myths and challenge stereotypes; to encourage disabled women to believe in themselves as parents; and to demonstrate that those who do not parent, whether by choice or by force of circumstances, are equally relevant to this debate. The title *Bigger than the Sky* reflects the way in which contributors are exploring their dreams and challenging rigid, limiting views of both what it means to be a disabled woman, and of what a parent is and does.

In Adina Frieden's piece, she describes how her access to biological motherhood was prematurely terminated when a surgeon fulfilled her wish to be sterilised on the grounds that she 'didn't want to pollute the gene pool' and how, years later, she identified and bitterly regretted the assumptions that caused the health professionals to go along with such a request. Yet, despite her experiences, Adina found her own access to parenting through her involvement in the life of a friend's young son: 'I think about how my experiences with Justin are like a unique constellation of parenthood; different from others, but still just as amazing. I realize I attained these experiences because I learned to move past limiting images of both parenthood and disability.'

In another contribution, 'Until Now' by Alana Theriault, we are given a piece of writing in which the author considers that she might be pregnant. What the outcome of the situation is we never learn, nor does it matter in the context of the writing because the strength of Alana's piece is her acknowledgement that pregnancy and parenting are options that are open to her and, in recognising that fact, she breaks through a societal taboo and a psychological barrier.

Piece after piece throws off the weight of other people's assumptions and the fear of being seen as we truly are. To be able to describe one's own experience, whether it is with the evident self-confidence in a job that is going well or whether it is from within situations that are painful, unresolved and even confusing, is a tremendously powerful thing to do. It is like shining a beacon in a storm; an offer of safety to all that see it.

But the safety offered by this anthology is not one of asserting that everything will turn out all right in the end; it is the safety of being able to explore where we are now, where we have come from and where we are going as disabled women. The story of a woman struggling is the story of a woman on a journey and nowhere is this more evident than in the moving and candid piece by Jodi Hoar, in which she explores her own perceptions of what being a disabled woman means both for her and for the children she is parenting on her own. Jodi acknowledges that for a long time she has been 'a person struggling not to think of herself as disabled' but, by the end of her piece, she recognises the limitations that this struggle has placed upon herself and her children: 'My reluctance to accept the disability label, my resistance to talking about the ongoing blending of parental expectations with the needs of a disabled person, is unfair to both them and me. Our energy might be better spent coming to terms with this unique and formative reality rather than dreaming about a different one.'

On a larger scale, this powerful, exciting, often painful journey is clearly demonstrated by Corbett Joan O'Toole as she describes the way in which generations of disabled people 'have suffered greatly to have even the hint of an independent "normal" life'. She acknowledges that those who came before us 'left home and blazed a trail in a new world' and goes on to describe Meecha, her disabled daughter, as 'the second generation child who gets to remember the old ways – and learns from the new – a child of both countries'.

As disabled women ourselves we have been aware of the temptation to avoid pieces in which the writer does not, or cannot, celebrate the situation that she finds herself in, for fear of reinforcing the negative attitudes of those who criticise the choices we make for ourselves. For many of us, it is frightening and dangerous to acknowledge what is perceived to be weakness, vulnerability and even failure. As Jo Litwinowicz explains: 'I didn't dare tell anyone how I was feeling in case they took my son away. I didn't even tell my husband, and so it just stayed bottled inside me.'

Speaking out about difficult situations and complex emotions does create risks, but as editors of what we believe is a groundbreaking book, we wanted to 'tell it as it really is'; to document where disabled women are today in the belief that the breadth of experience is important to the story as a whole. As Liz Crow states in *Encounters With Strangers* (ed. Jenny Morris), the 'suppression of our subjective experiences' is not the answer to dealing with the risks involved.

Audre Lorde, a Black lesbian poet who lived with cancer for several years before her death, stated: 'While we wait in silence for that final luxury of fearlessness, the weight of that silence will choke us.' Until now, silence has played a quiet, but significantly undermining and destructive, role in the relationship between disabled women and parenting. This anthology contains many examples of that silence in the lives of contributors; from the silence of health professionals who provide nothing by way of pre-pregnancy advice but appear on the scene at the discovery of pregnancy and urge disabled women to have abortions; to the silence that disabled mothers feel constrained to keep when facing difficulties, for fear that someone will take their children away.

Karen Peterson Butterworth explains how vulnerable

she felt, as a disabled, single mother in 1950s New Zealand, who wanted to keep her baby rather than have it adopted: 'The social worker said, "Well it's plain you want to keep your baby. Let's work out how." When I had recovered from my tears of relief we worked out a plan of action, but I didn't tell her about my polio. I thought that would stretch her tolerance too far.'

Perhaps the most significant silence of all is illustrated by Alicia Contreras' piece, in which the mother of a disabled 19-year-old asks, 'Why should I talk about sexuality with my daughter?' That mother does not consider such a conversation to be relevant because it has never occurred to her that her daughter could be sexually desirable to anyone. As Alicia points out, 'If that is what you think of her, then that is what she will believe.'

Unfortunately, Alicia (and others like her) cannot speak to all mothers and there are many disabled women throughout the world for whom parenting remains at most an unfulfilled dream. There are others who have not felt free even to dream of parenting and whose feelings on this subject remain unexpressed. Countless disabled women of earlier generations were prevented from parenting by institutionalisation, compulsory sterilisations or enforced adoptions, and we are acutely aware of these untold stories.

Nowhere is the breaking of silence, the power of telling it like it is, more evident than in Jo Litwinowicz's epic piece, 'In My Mind's Eye'. Her strength and persistence in the face of some of the most blatant examples of prejudice and misinformed practice are striking. Jo's writing captures the creative spirit in which a disabled woman, clear in her own mind about the challenges and barriers facing her, uses humour, anger, skilled strategic planning and irrepressible resourcefulness to succeed in the task of parenting. There is so much in Jo's description, from the difficulty of getting pre-pregnancy advice, through to enlisting allies to assist her in enriching her son's life, that we felt this piece merited its position in sections throughout the book.

One of the most startling, although perhaps not entirely surprising, themes within many pieces we received, was the notion of producing a 'perfect' child. We had, perhaps somewhat naively, assumed that the majority of disabled women would be 'beyond' the desire to parent the most beautiful, most healthy, most gifted child. Often the author's assumptions in this respect were at odds with what was said elsewhere in the piece. One writer who worked with this contradiction was Ellen Basani in 'A Damned Good Job': 'When my baby was given to me and my fingers traced dully over his perfectly formed body, they came to rest on his head. Horrified, my hands recoiled. The forehead, which I had expected to be smooth and well rounded, felt jagged and deformed. Could I have given birth to a monster?' Finally Ellen makes the connection between early experiences of rejection and her initial response to her baby: 'How could I love in another human being that which I most feared and rejected in myself – physical imperfection?'

These are difficult feelings to discuss and Ellen's honesty is valuable. We live, grow, learn and survive in a world that does not celebrate difference and we, like any parents, naturally long for our children to be celebrated. Most parents, disabled or not, can empathise with Corbett Joan O'Toole when she writes of Meecha, her daughter, and describes one of the hardest parts of parenting her as 'knowing that the world will hurt her for being disabled and being powerless to prevent that hurt'. As disabled women, we have all experienced that hurt in various forms and would certainly not wish it on our own children.

However, Corbett is one of a number of disabled women within this anthology who have actively sought out and celebrated the experience of parenting a disabled child. From both biological and adoptive mothers we have wonderful examples of Disability Pride being passed down from one generation to the next. As we write, the 'problem' of genetic inheritance is being hotly debated by ethics committees, impairment based charities, Disabled Peoples' Organisations and geneticists worldwide. For many of us, the increase in the availability of pre-natal screening that inevitably leads to an increase in the number of abortions performed on the grounds of impairment, denies our cultural identity and devalues our individual lives. The ongoing search for 'cures' and the widespread availability of medical and surgical intervention are all adding to the pressure on disabled people to conform to a non-disabled notion of 'normality'. Our future existence as disabled women is under threat and so, for many of us, it is comforting to know that all over the world, disabled women are creating and celebrating disabled children.

From the outset, we felt that this anthology would find its own shape. We hoped that it would be possible to include writing from women outside of Britain but we certainly didn't envisage the breadth of writing that has reached us from around the world. It has become a truly diverse collection. Largely through use of the Internet and partly by our presence at the first international conference on the subject of Parenting and Disability, held in California in October 1997, we have enjoyed dialogues with disabled women throughout the world.

Insights from different cultures have given us the opportunity to both reinforce the common nature of our experience as disabled women and also highlight some different perspectives. Rosangela Berman Bieler's perspective on Europe as a visiting outsider is particularly thought-provoking: 'On a trip to Europe, one disabled woman asked me what I had to do to get my doctor's approval for my pregnancy...She told me that the doctors there were very controlling and even discouraged disabled women from having children. I assume this happens because of a lack of information and the prejudice of some doctors, not on the basis of actual medical risk.'

Piecing together a collection by disabled women with

diverse experiences and backgrounds created a number of challenges for us as editors. We had women writing in their second and third languages, we had women with little experience or knowledge of writing and we had relatively few resources available to accommodate the needs of individual writers. We had to set boundaries that inevitably made it difficult for some groups of women to contribute. We are aware of the limitations this has placed on both those who have contributed and those who have not.

Despite these limitations, however, we have been delighted by the diversity and range of experiences described by the disabled women who have submitted their work. In reality, the way in which disability is traditionally viewed through the Medical Model, as a series of distinct and distinguishable medical, psychological or cognitive conditions which are attached to individuals, and to groups of individuals who have been allotted the same label, is extremely misleading. It masks both the commonality of our experience as disabled women and the uniqueness of our experience as individuals. In this anthology, as in our lives, we have rejected this Medical Model definition of disability and have followed the Social Model, which defines disability as a social construction. It takes a holistic approach, viewing us in our wider contexts and, in doing so, liberates us from the damaging and inaccurate belief that we are the problem, that it is us, as disabled women, who are responsible for the difficulties experienced as a result of our needs. Viewing those difficulties through the Social Model enables us to see that the roots of our problems stem from social environments, attitudes and the institutional mechanisms that are not designed to accommodate our needs and differences.

Time after time we read how the discomfort and fear of others affects the choices available to disabled women regardless of their 'medical' impairment; and piece after piece relates the difficulties experienced by disabled mothers, purely through the inappropriate design of childcare equipment or the inadequate provision of support services. For example, Jill Daly writes that 'there was no child car seat on the British market that I could use', and in 'Enmeshed' Vicky D'aoust explains that 'because we are Deaf we are far more restricted in who we can turn to for help...we had a lot of trouble trying to find a therapist and counsellor who would be able to communicate with both Marianne and me and who would also understand my disability'. It is the realisation, often gained through support groups and the Disability Rights Movement, that such experiences are common to disabled people throughout the world, that begins to break the oppression of isolation.

The range of experiences described within this collection illustrates the truth that anyone can become disabled regardless of culture, birth situation or chosen lifestyle. We also wanted the rich diversity of disabled women to be reflected, not just in content, but also in style. For that reason we have chosen to retain country-specific spellings and terminology, individual writers' preferred use of capitalisation and, where we deemed necessary for the expression of individual experiences, words that we would not ourselves use. We have maintained a commitment to editing for clarity of communication rather than grammatical convention and, in so doing, believe that the women's voices can be heard as clearly as is possible within the confines of a written publication.

So, as editors, we have had the privilege of weaving a wonderful tapestry from threads that have come to us from all over the world. We have only been able to include a proportion of writings submitted and, whilst it has not been possible to cover every parenting issue that is experienced by disabled women, we have attempted to create a map of strengths and experiences that have inspired and excited us. As readers, we hope that you too will be inspired, whether as a professional who has the power to change oppressive practices, as a non-disabled individual who has the potential to become a proactive ally or, perhaps most importantly, as a disabled woman, for whom the choices, dreams and realities of parenting really can be limitless.

Rowen Jade and Michele Wates

Acknowledgements

We would like to thank all the disabled women who submitted work for us to consider; their support, understanding and cooperation throughout the editing process have been invaluable. We are particularly grateful to those who spent time and energy rewriting their pieces.

As co-editors, we would like to acknowledge each other and the considerable efforts we have both made to the process of working in partnership. It has been challenging, stimulating, fascinating and fun. We also acknowledge the very considerable support and editorial skills of Kirsty Dunseath at The Women's Press, whose enthusiasm for this anthology has been a great encouragement. Finally, we would like to acknowledge and thank families and friends who have given support throughout. With particular thanks to Jaz, Edward, Anna and David.

ACKNOWLEDGEMENTS

Part I
Making Plans

Until Now

Alana Theriault

I'm 30 years old and this is the first time I've had to wonder if I am indeed pregnant. I keep counting the days on my calendar since I last bled...43...44...45...46...and can't help but notice how tender my breasts are. My 45-pound, scoliosed body has never bled regularly for more than six months at a time, so is not a dependable measure. I'm exhausted. I'm sleepy. I'm emotional. I'm all of those pre-menstrual things without the menstrual part of the deal coming forth. I'm on the unforgiving mini-pill and I did the unforgivable. I missed a day and had sex.

My fragile body and I have been negotiating with my love to learn how close we can be. We learned a lot. He says he has a low sperm count. I say the women in my family are baby machines. Am I a baby machine, too? I need help to care for myself in even the smallest ways. Can I care for someone else? Is this little body of mine meant to create another little body? Joy leaps into my throat and chokes me as I cram the excitement back down to where I hope a baby is not. The ache in my spine crashes through my thoughts; the spine that cannot support my own weight, and could not bear the weight of another, no matter how small.

And then I wonder, 'Is there a way?' And I picture holding a small child between me and my partner, all of us napping with dreams of our future. Would I be a good mother? Could I even hold a baby with my so thin arms in a way that makes it feel safe and completely loved?

As a ventilator pushes air deep into my lungs, I wonder if I could even breathe with a baby growing inside me. I can hardly breathe after eating half a burrito. Could I with-stand months of bedrest, knowing that each day I would lose more of my reach, a wiggle of a finger, the turn of my head, a shoulder shrugging? These are the small, precious things my body can now do. Is it a fair trade, these things for a precious life? Will that baby be granted my own physical limitations as a genetic bonus prize? Will I be destined to live on public assistance? Will I have to quit my job and struggle to get us both up in the morning? Will my lover always be gone to make money and too tired to be my love? If he wants to stay home and I want to work, will I be able to sit upright long enough to enjoy all the parts of my life?

All of these questions have been easy to answer until now.

Insemination

Rowen Jade

Insemination. A word, a clinical act, a two second process that fits neatly between sips of hot tea. And as I pay the price of a possible baby, we smile in the knowledge that my Disability Living Allowance was not intended for this way of living.

As my tea cools, my girlfriend gently rocks from side to side, encouraging an even distribution of the precious seminal fluid. This is my choice and it feels right, to be in this clinic with the woman I love, creating a child who will carry my name and know me as 'Mum'. We talk about eggs in the hope that our attention will encourage conception, but I quickly catch myself wondering how fertile my own eggs are right now. Our cycles are synchronised and a gentle ache on my left side is urging me to look at the kidney dish. The vial is empty, although I'm sure I can see a small drop at the end, perhaps not enough for a child but enough for a tiny sensation of possible chance to rush through my body and ferment in my mind.

But I've made my choice and I'm committed to being here with my girlfriend, supporting her body to nurture and grow. To chance my own body would be a momentous risk; it could end all our plans, our future, my life. It could prevent me from breathing and it would be virtually impossible to lift my increased weight. My food intake, already a struggle, would need to be doubled at least. I don't need to be pregnant and I certainly don't want to die.

Together, we picture a choir of all kinds of people pushing their way to the front of the crowd. Which one will win? Which is the sperm that will enter the egg and what is it like and who will it be? I picture the tortoise being trampled by hares and hope it survives to the end of the race.

We talk about names. Nothing biblical, traditional or too way out. Our child will face judgements enough without the added hurdle of being called Starburst or Galaxy Jade. So we think alphabetically about people we've known and talk about harsh sounds, soft sounds and various connotations. After Ashton, Briony and Charlie, I remember Drucilla and recall the convictions that her name still evokes.

We were five and a half but the new intake at Christmas made us feel like adults. We were planning our futures in the playground and Drucilla the Dancer asked me what I intended to do with my life. I proudly declared that I would be having a baby and that the bank was going to pay me lots of money for being a mother. She stood up, tried to perform a plié and then explained that I was stupid because no boys would love me enough to give me their babies. Had I not been a wheelchair user with a very powerful adult sized chair at this point, I might have pulled Drucilla's hair or pushed her into the ditch at the bottom of the playground where the sticky dragons lived. Instead, my instinct was to head towards her, into her, and continue moving forwards until we reached the wall. I was in fourth gear and Drucilla didn't know how to turn my chair off. She was screaming but my voice was growing louder than hers: 'I will be a Mummy, they will love me, they will and I'll show you!'

And now we are showing them, my girlfriend and I. Every time we come to the clinic, as we sit on the steps waiting for the ramps to be found, we show them. We pass the Harley Street waiting room where my presence is questioned by looks of pity mingled with fear, and I feel the panic rising in gold embossed women as they realise that their money might not be enough to buy their way out of conceiving someone like me.

And I show them all, as we are ushered into the lift

ahead of the queue. My choice has been made by no one but me and whether our child is conceived this month, next, or perhaps not at all, I show them that my chances and choices are real.

A Few Thoughts About Children

Wendy S Harbour

There's something wonderful about not having children. Don't get me wrong – I've thought a lot about having kids. Sometimes, late at night, lying in bed after watching *Full House* re-runs, I want to have children just as much as any deaf lesbian ever could. My biological clock is ticking away and I just know that any second I'm going to wake up in the middle of menopause, deciding between soy nuts and estrogen pills to cure my hot flashes and knowing that my childbearing days are over.

Choosing to live as an honest-to-goddess lesbian used to mean that everything was decided in the baby department and you never had to worry about taking down the neutral wallpaper in the guest room and replacing it with something that had bunnies on it. The only way you ended up being a Mom was if you hooked up with somebody who already had a kid. The only other way was to start off as a straight mom – to be at a PTA fundraiser in the park wearing a wedding ring, and then suddenly realize you want to run off with the PTA secretary.

My child-free friends and I take great pride in pointing out that we can go flying off to Bermuda at any time, have sex on the kitchen floor in the middle of the day, keep toxic plants all over the house, and stay out until 3 a.m. whenever we feel like it. We mention the escalating world population and how we refuse to contribute to it. Putting on our intellectual thinking caps, we sit in coffee shops and ponder whether lesbians unconsciously seek validation from straight culture through our reproductive capabilities. Wallets open and out come pictures of pets: 'No squalling child could ever replace Sappho – she's the cutest little spaniel this side of the Mississippi!'

On the other hand, I have friends who have wanted kids and are: (a) dealing with the little munchkins now and marching in the 'WE LOVE OUR FAMILIES' part of the annual Pride March; (b) trying to decide how to get the sperm into their bodies (the old 'penis *vs.* turkey baster' debate); (c) figuring out which partner has better child-bearing hips and a higher pain tolerance; or (d) fighting their way through a maze of adoption procedures. All of them seem really happy with their momhood (whether current or impending) and expound the joys of raising kids who are open-minded, loved and cared about. Some of them had (or have) problems with grandparents not really accepting their kids. Some of them have kids who are...umm...less than angelic in their behavior. Bumps and bruises and daily dramas come and go. In other words, they encompass the range of straight families I know, and their kids seem as happy as any others.

That's the lesbian community. Then I've got my pals in the disability and deaf communities. Here the Moms are fewer, for a variety of reasons. Money definitely plays a part. It's hard to have kids when you're struggling to find work and convince the Government that $452.63 per month is not enough for rent, food and medicine. It's also tough to have discussions about children with doctors when they ignore the fact that we even have sex lives. 'My doctor was about to put me on a new med,' a wheelchair-using friend with epilepsy told me, 'And he asked me if I plan to have children. I didn't know what to say. No doctor's asked me that before. I've always had to bring it up.' Sometimes it's tough just to get past the birth control in our heads; the little thoughts and fears and stereotypes about our own disabilities that make us wonder if we'll ever make decent moms. 'What if my pain is so bad I can't pick up my own child?' 'What if I kill myself while I'm pregnant because I stop taking my psych meds?' 'What if something goes wrong in labor because of my disability and there's nobody to take care of my new baby?' And then the worst one of all (because it's so real, so politically difficult and gives voice to so many personal and cultural demons): 'What if my baby has a disability, too?'

Those are questions I don't see deaf women asking. There are deaf pre-natal classes, deaf childcare classes and interpreters who specialize in medical interpreting and are able to go into the delivery room. Deaf women take things into their own hands and sometimes try to genetically engineer the results to get a deaf baby. (One fourth-generation deaf man I know has been repeatedly asked for sperm and isn't sure whether to be embarrassed or flattered.) With a current trend towards 'fixing' deafness and mainstreaming deaf kids to be as hearing and integrated as possible, the deaf community is watching its own slow extinction. The community's urge to propagate itself and raise beloved deaf children who cherish sign language and their deaf community is as strong as my lesbian friends' urge to have sons and daughters with open minds who see beyond sexual labels. A sense of pride in who we are carries over into a sense of pride in ourselves as mothers. Whether you are disabled, deaf, lesbian, a person of color, or a member of any similarly oppressed group, you know that your children will crawl forward with the weight of the world like lead in their diaper. The only way to ease their burden is to raise children for the future – children of possibility.

If I were deaf and straight, I might be interviewing interpreters for the delivery room. If I were a hearing lesbian, I might be deciding between sperm donor #45033 and #56071. But I'm a deaf lesbian. Hmm...

I don't really know many deaf or disabled lesbians who have children. At the moment, I can only think of one who is even considering it. I am firmly convinced that if I ever decide to remodel my guest room with a bunny theme, adoption is the way to go for me. Right this exact second though, I'm much happier having sex on the kitchen floor once in a while. I'm not interested in having a child right now and have a hard time articulating the reasons without annoying myself or sounding hypocritical. I used to say that it wasn't fair to impose my lifestyle on a child; to ask them to face the prejudices of society. But then what about people of color? They face prejudice, and no one would suggest they stop having kids. Any person who doesn't want to know me or my child because of where the sperm came from, or who I sleep with, or the fact we wear matching mom/baby Birkenstock sandals . . . that's not a person I want my child hanging out with anyway. And as for my 'lifestyle', here's a thought: I've decided to be a meat-eater. What if my child turns out to be a vegetarian at age four telling me to eat my broccoli because it's good for me? There's a huge lifestyle clash, because I really love my Cajun chicken sandwiches, darn it. What if they decide to become a Buddhist? What if they want to move to Brazil? What if they become a right-wing Republican? Lifestyle is merely a matter of definition and is inherently unique for each individual. My mother shared her values, beliefs and culture with me, but ultimately I had to decide whether to accept or reject them. That's a Truth for each generation and every family.

My 'pros' and 'cons' list has items which seem to cancel each other out. Ultimately, I think that's the way it will always be. I can easily picture myself as a 75-year-old woman, sitting on a park bench watching my grand-children play, thinking how silly all this deep thoughtful questioning was. I can just as easily picture myself sitting on that park bench watching other people's grand-children playing, thinking how glad I am that the only pictures in my wallet are of my dog.

I guess I believe that motherhood is a 'calling' – just like a person gets to go into seminary, explore the Himalayas, or enter the Indy 500. To have a baby just for me, with everything revolving around how I feel and how everything will affect me . . . that's selfish. When the baby (or an older child needing adoption) calls out to me; when there's some little tug inside that says there's a mom waiting to get out and a really terrific kid in my future;

when my friends talk about their children (or freedom from children) and I respond with 'Uh, huh' because it doesn't matter what the hell they think; when I start planning what I'll wear to my lesbian deaf daughter's presidential inauguration ceremony...that's when I'll start looking for the perfect turkey baster, register for one of those deaf parenting classes, and start hunting for a smaller apartment while cutting up credit cards.

If you need me before then, I'll be looking at travel brochures for Bermuda while eating a Cajun chicken sandwich.

Fertility Goddess
a sestina

Laura Hershey

Her five-dollar yardsale price tag does nothing
(we hope) to diminish the quiet power
residing in her beads and cowrie shells, in her smooth
   round shape.
We bring her home, dust her a little; we stand
her on a molding over the dining room door
to the extra bedroom. She is real, in the sense of real
   wood.

The realness of her divinity remains
to be seen; but there's almost nothing
we won't try, now, to get through that door
guarded by the Department of Social Services' powers
that be. Sternly, rulebook in hand, they stand
admitting or denying entrance. Judging by the shape

of us, by our wheelchairs, they decide we are in no shape
to supervise young children. How on earth would
we rescue them from fires, from soiled beds? One of us
   cannot stand;
the other barely walks. We are outraged: Knowing
   nothing
about us, how dare they use their power
to shut, to lock, this door?

We appeal. Under hinted threat of suit, they send
a social worker to our door.
Cheerfully, she fills out forms; inspects the size and
   shape
of the extra bedroom. She compliments our hardwood

floors; our educational achievements; the generous
  power
of our desire. "God wants you to have a child,"
she says. (To this we say nothing.
We will smile, for now; play their games; and prepare to
  take a stand

when we must.) During the interview, our fertility
  goddess stands
watching, listening, from her perch above the door.
Unlike the social worker's God, our goddess wants
  nothing, directs nothing.
She doesn't work that way.
Instead, she waits, carrying the weight and shape
of what we want. All our hope and doubt gestates
in the dense wood of her body. With the power

she brought along, pent-up and palpable, she nourishes
  the force
of our dreams. For years she waited, displayed on an old
  man's shelf
or bookstand, never called upon, never impregnated; a
  mere artifact.
Finally, one hot Saturday, we carried her through our
  door
to play a part in the drama just starting to take shape
in our lives, which might lead to nothing –

our hearts broken, our power wasted by a system
that would rather bar its door to us than find a child a
  home –
or might, after all, let us shape
and cherish a child, teach her to stand proud
and let the world deny her nothing.

Discussing Sexuality with Disabled Girls

Alicia Contreras

Note sent to an international e-mail network of Disabled women

Dear everyone!

Today I went to the meeting of the MD Association [the Muscular Dystrophy Association]. It was a beautiful day and when I arrived the kids were outside playing on the grass. Before going to say hello to them, there was a support group of their parents having a meeting and I went to watch. Guess what? The leader of the group was discussing the importance of parents talking about sexuality with their kids. I was very silent, listening and wondering if all the parents were thinking about discussing sexuality with their disabled kids or just with their other kids.

Well ... I finally decided to speak up and said, 'Excuse me for my ignorance. I do know a little tiny bit about sexuality for people who are paraplegic and can't feel in some parts of the body but can have orgasms, thanks to other parts of their bodies being more sensitive; bearing in mind, for example, that the biggest "organ" in our bodies is the skin. Do you have information about sexuality for people who have MD?'

As I guessed, some of the parents had never thought about the sexuality of their disabled kids and there was one woman who immediately said, 'Why should I talk about sexuality with my daughter?'

Some other parents were surprised and the leader did not know what to say, so she said, 'I will let Alicia answer you.'

To tell the truth I was shocked! All the parents were

listening and looking at me and I asked this woman, 'Why shouldn't you provide this information for your daughter?'

She said, 'What for? Nobody would want to marry her!'

Me: 'If that is what you think of her, then that is what she will believe. Do you think that I can be a mother?'

She: 'Yes.'

Me: 'What's the difference between your daughter and me?'

She: 'You can walk with crutches and she is in a wheelchair.'

Me: 'Does a woman need to walk to have a baby? How old is your daughter?'

She: 'Nineteen years old.'

Me: 'Does she have her period every month?' (Of course you can imagine the red faces, especially the fathers!)

She: 'Yes.'

Me: 'Don't you think that that is enough to prove that she does have a body like any other woman and that she can be a mother like anybody else? Don't you think that she should learn about her sexuality? Do you all know that the highest rate of rape is among women with disabilities, and that part of the problem is that few disabled people have access to information about sexuality and that's why they are so often the victims of sexual abuse?'

The woman turned her body around to avoid looking at me, trying to escape, but at least some parents agreed that their kids should learn about this topic.

I hope you all have a good day.

Regards,

Alicia Contreras
Mexico
1 March 1998

The Secret

Jenni Meredith

Her eyes sparkle beneath the medicated lids. 'I've got a secret,' they say. No one notices. She goes to buy some food. Several cars pass her on the way to the baker's. No one inside them looks at her. They don't know. They would have looked had they known she had a secret. They would have wound down the windows and waved, wanting to share it with her. But they don't know. So she smiles instead. Her smile tells them she has a secret. If only they had the time to read it. But they speed off in their Rovers past the wandering figure in the tie-dyed T-shirt and flower-trimmed denims... Dash off to their offices and important meetings. She arrives at the baker's and stands in the queue fidgeting, smiles and nods at the others queuing ahead. They ignore her for the most part, though one mother with two loudly happy children smiles back absently, her mind calculating weekly shopping bills and whether there is enough today for a cup cake each. Perhaps she understands?

At the head of the queue now she turns to speak to the woman behind the counter. She wants to shout out her news... To tell the world. But she can't... it's a secret. So she asks for a split tin loaf instead.

It's later now and her eyes are heavier. The epanutims fill her head with mashed potato. Life orbits her leisurely space too fast and too frantically for her to keep concentration or even to stay conscious. She sleeps. And dreams. Dreams of motherhood.

Waiting on the hard chairs wedged between a chest cough and a backache, she smiles that twinkling 'I've got a

27

secret' smile. But the chest cough simply wheezes and the backache shifts her weight to the other buttock. 'If only they knew,' she thinks and regards them with a deep and sincere sympathy. 'They think I'm here because I'm ill too. If only they knew...' She smiles inwardly and in her head sees the wheezing, creaky patients stand to applaud her. The dew-nosed infant and the red-eyed alcoholic in the corner clap and cheer with the rest as she marches triumphantly out of the surgery, officially pregnant...

She rehearses internally...'I think I'm pregnant...I'm having a baby...I'm overdue so...' None of them sounds right. She isn't sure how to word it. She is sure, though, that the doctor will be as pleased as she is with the news...

'Well, are you married?' he glowers. Doesn't deserve an answer, that. I come here with a secret I've been bursting all day to share and what do I get? Insults, prejudice...

'Of course,' she smiles.

'Even so, you shouldn't have done it,' he adds sternly, as he peruses the browning record sheets.

'Why not?'

'Well, you're epileptic, aren't you?...Anyway, you just make sure you don't ever get pregnant again...'

Her eyes are in flames beneath the medicated lids. 'I'm angry and hurt, but you can't destroy me that easily,' they say to anyone who has the time to read them. She walks home past the library and several cars pass her. If the people inside their Rovers and Austins had turned their heads as they passed, they would have noticed the determined figure in the shabby sweater and flower-trimmed denims.

In My Mind's Eye: I
Pre-pregnancy and becoming pregnant

Jo Litwinowicz

Ever since I can remember, I've dreamt of being married and having at least six children. I was born with cerebral palsy which makes my right hand and leg do involuntary movements. My speech was very hard to understand until I had a brain operation at the age of 16, which I think has made it easier. As a child I spent more time in hospital than at home, so in some ways I felt more at ease in hospital. Also, my younger brother didn't get picked on so much when I was away.

When I was 22 I decided that I didn't want to go through life 'holding mummy's apron strings', so I went to live in a village specially equipped so that disabled and able-bodied people could live and work together. A couple of years later I met my husband who lived in the same hostel. He is much older than me and came to the village as a TB patient which left him with a very weak chest and one lung.

About three months before our wedding I made an appointment to talk to the doctor about going on the pill. Even though my husband and I both loved children, we thought it would be wrong to bring a child into the world if that child was going to suffer because I couldn't do things like other mums and my husband couldn't run around like other dads.

But deep down, I still hoped we would have a child.

The doctor told us that as my husband was on all kinds of medication he didn't think he would be able to father a child, and it was unlikely that I could have children, but he'd make an appointment for us to see the Family Planning Clinic. He said the pill would be unsuitable for me and told us not to worry about contraception for the moment. We got an appointment through to see Family Planning but it was fourteen weeks after our wedding so, even though the doctor had told us not to bother, we still took our own precautions.

As the date for our appointment grew nearer, I was beginning to panic. Secretly I wanted to get pregnant and felt as if I was waving goodbye to my dream. I also felt really rough and thought I had food poisoning. After another week, I still hadn't shaken it off so I went to see the doctor. Our doctor was on holiday, so I saw his partner who asked me if I could be pregnant. I didn't think so. Still he took my sample and told me to come back on Friday for the result. I didn't tell my husband about the test as I didn't want him to get excited unnecessarily. On the Friday I woke up feeling dizzy and ill. As my husband worked opposite the surgery I asked him to get the result of a test I had done. I told him to go in at 11 a.m. and if the receptionist said that it was negative then he should go back to work, but if it was positive, I wanted him to come straight home.

By 11.30 he hadn't come back, so I decided I couldn't be pregnant, which I had suspected all along, but I still felt disappointed. When he came home at 12.30 I was preparing dinner. I was facing the hob and I didn't dare look at him. I said, 'Did you remember to go to the surgery for me?' He didn't answer so I turned round and there was a wide grin on his face. 'Hello little mum,' he said.

When he had gone to the surgery, the doctor had come out of his room and shook his hand saying, 'Congratulations, how do you feel, being a dad-to-be?' When he recovered from the shock my husband went back to work and told his mates. On the way home he met some of my friends and told them the great news and they said that I must be over the moon, at which point my husband said, 'Oh God, I forgot to tell my own wife she's expecting.' Still, in this house we like to do things differently.

When the news had sunk in, my husband and I sat down and had a serious talk. We knew it was going to be an uphill struggle to convince the authorities that we could manage and we knew that they would put obstacles in our way. We had already talked about all the pitfalls in caring for a child and we wanted this child so much, but the biggest step was getting the doctors, social workers and everyone else on our side. We wanted them to understand that we were going into this with our eyes wide open. Once we'd achieved that, half the battle would be won.

By Sunday we had got used to the fact that we were going to become parents, so we went down to the phone box to ring my mum and dad. I said to mum, 'How would you like to be a gran?' There was silence for what seemed an eternity. I heard mum calling dad to the phone and she asked me to repeat what I had said so I told them that I was expecting. Their reaction devastated me. 'Well Jo, that news has turned this day into a tragic day. You are an irresponsible and stupid girl.' They might as well have kicked me in my stomach; I was so upset that I slammed the phone down. If my parents' reaction was bad, what chance did we have with complete strangers?

When I went to see my doctor at his antenatal clinic his first words to me were, 'God, you were the last person I thought I'd see down here.' 'Sorry to disappoint you,' I replied. He asked how we felt about the prospect of becoming parents, and we told him that deep down we had both secretly pined for a child and it was the greatest news ever. His response was to say that throughout my pregnancy, if ever I wanted an abortion he could arrange it. I was totally horrified and said it would NEVER be an option, even if they found that something was wrong with the baby. We were disabled and could cope with a disabled child. Didn't he think we should have a choice? Didn't he think we're capable of *thinking for ourselves*? Just because I'm in a wheelchair and can't use my limbs properly it shouldn't automatically exclude me from the happiness of having a child of my own.

I was so livid with the doctor. He said, 'You can get off the soapbox now, but please go and think about what I said,' so I replied, 'If you'll think about what I said.'

The next day there was a knock on the door and this woman said she was from Family Planning and could she come in for a chat. I joked, 'You're a bit too late'. She went on, saying how hard it was going to be to raise a child and told me I couldn't possibly manage in my condition. I said, 'What condition? You don't know me and what I'm capable of. For your information I'll manage like any mother. Nobody knows how to bring up a child till it's there. Everyone's different and I will have different problems and I'll be ready for them when they crop up and I'll solve them like any parent.' She said, 'Well, you won't consider an abortion then?' I said 'NO WAY!'

She calmly went on, 'You do realise that when your child can walk and talk it will come to you and say, "I hate you mother because you can't talk properly, you dribble and you're in a wheelchair and I want a new mother."' I began to see red and if my husband hadn't come in, I dread to think what I'd have done to that woman! He opened the door wide and explained that he had heard what was said; 'For your information we WANT THIS BABY. Get out of our home and don't come upsetting my wife, except to apologise, but do make an appointment first. If you were so concerned that we couldn't look after a child why didn't you come and see us sooner, before we got married?' She said, 'I was very busy,' and my husband remarked, 'Not too busy to rush down here to tell us to get rid of our baby.' I was in a terrible state.

The doctor came up to see us three hours later. He said, 'What have you been up to, upsetting all the professional people now!' We told him our version and he was most apologetic. We spent two hours discussing the situation and how we felt. We really thrashed it out and then the doctor said, 'Well you've thought it through and you've convinced me. From now on I'll do everything in my power to help you.' I cried with joy that we actually had our doctor on side at last. True to his word, he was a tower of strength for us and will always be a dear friend.

Child

Sue Napolitano

Before, so many unused rooms.
No light, no air, no warmth,
Just the dankness of bare neglected brick
And crumbling plaster,
Doors shut so long they'd forgotten how to open.

And then you came,
Pushed head first into the world.
Bloody.
Your first cry soon forgotten as you found
Warm tummy,
And a breast,
And how to get the milk out
And then my arms
And sleep.

And already you had started to push at the first door.
I felt it squealing on its hinges,
Reluctant to shift, but shifting none the less,
The merest crack,
But still, it stirred the air inside a little,
Allowed a little sharing of light
Between cramped spaces.
It had begun.

The Right to Maternity

Rosangela Berman Bieler

At the age of 19, in Rio de Janeiro, where I was born, I had a car accident and became quadriplegic. A year later, in 1977, I got involved in the Brazilian Disability Rights Movement, advocating through a 'patients' club' inside the rehabilitation centre, and from that point on, I became totally committed to the cause. Right after the accident, I decided to restart college and got my degree in social communications, majoring in advertising and journalism. I met my husband at University and studied with him for 4 years. Our daughter Mel was born in 1986 and is now a beautiful teenager.

At that time in Brazil, few women with severe disabilities had the opportunity to experience maternity, at least few that we knew of. There were probably many other disabled women who had passed through the health system to have their babies but there was no data available. We faced a major lack of information about disability amongst doctors and rehabilitation service providers; for example, *I* was the one who provided information to my gynaecologist on spinal cord injury issues. In general, the gynaecologists and obstetricians didn't know much about disability and pregnancy, and were not used to dealing with it.

At the beginning of my pregnancy, we visited a prestigious rehabilitation centre for spinal cord injuries in Stoke Mandeville, England. I had heard that the founder, Dr Gutmann, had conducted some research on maternity and women with disabilities. We brought selected texts back to Brazil and translated them into Portuguese to study with my doctor, who happened to be a woman, and who ended up becoming a close friend of ours.

Unfortunately, to my doctor's despair, I developed all the complications that can happen to a quadriplegic during pregnancy. However, I have friends with spinal cord injuries who have had problem-free pregnancies. One of them had three children within a five year period! During pregnancy even her chronic urinary infection disappeared and she always felt in great shape. Had my husband and I planned to have a baby, maybe I could have avoided some of the problems that we faced. However, despite the tough moments during my pregnancy, I still feel the great pleasure of having generated inside my body a being, as a result of my love for my husband and of life itself.

I have learned from some women with disabilities that they also encountered a lack of information and support. On a trip to Europe, one disabled woman asked me what I had to do to get my doctor's approval for my pregnancy. I was surprised by that question and told her that I did not ask for permission to get pregnant. I just did it like everybody else. She told me that the doctors there were very controlling and even discouraged disabled women from having children. I assume this happens because of a lack of information and the prejudice of some doctors, not on the basis of actual medical risk.

We have to struggle in our daily lives to make society realise that we are women with the same instincts and rights as others. We also have to constantly educate doctors, who should be our allies but unfortunately are sometimes our greatest obstacle.

My relationship with my daughter when she was born was something full of beauty and strong emotion but there were difficulties too because, as well as her dependence on me, I was also physically dependent in some ways. I could not fulfil all her needs by myself – giving her a bath, changing her diapers and clothes, waking up in the middle of the night when she cried, running to save her from an emergency situation, feeding her with my own hands and so on.

It was a very hard experience for me because I had to share my motherhood with other people. On the other hand, we have always had a very strong emotional and affectionate relationship as mother and daughter, and this is something irreplaceable for both of us. I have learned that being able to be operationally efficient with a child is easily replaceable. I always tried to do as much as I could by myself or, when I couldn't, I stayed close by or actively directed my husband or my attendant on what to do and how to do it. In many ways, when she was little, my daughter's image of the 'mother-provider' was shared among a few close people. I don't know if this situation made her the independent person she is today or if it only reinforced her personal traits as an individual.

Well, now that she is a teenager, I am really happy with the results. I think my daughter has a healthy image of her mother, an image of a mother who is there for her, a regular mom. Last month, in school, her English teacher asked the students to describe a person in detail. She could have picked anyone but she chose to describe me:

> Rosangela Berman-Bieler is my mom. She has dark brown hair and light brown eyes. She loves to talk to her friends and family. My mom wears glasses and always has lipstick on. She always wears earrings no matter where she is. One thing my mom has that most people don't is a wheelchair. She was in a car accident when she was 19. Everyone thinks it is sad but she does not care. She is happy the way she is. My mom is a very caring person. She has a good humour and loves to laugh. She is a very nice person, too. But on the other side of the story she can be a pain. She, as you probably know, is like any other mother, sometimes pretty nice and sometimes pretty mean. But of course, I love her.

If you are a disabled woman, from any culture, with the desire to have or adopt a child, go ahead. It is your right. Of course you, as an adult and a responsible person, have

38 / Rosangela Berman Bieler

to be in control of this decision and evaluate when it is a medical risk. Don't leave this decision for somebody else to make or for society to judge. Take for yourself the very enjoyable responsibility of exploring all of your human and social roles.

Making A Reality of My Own

Liz Crow

Ho, Louis, my secular god son. Hey, little old man with your half-crown of hair edging the fontanelles of your birth. You in your jumpsuit, all rabbits and falling leaves, you are rocked, lulled to sweet, peaceful sleep. Small frowns chase across your forehead and your fists ball, fighting the air and creasing the plumpness of flesh.

Your eyes open to blink away dust. They swim with tears as that mouth opens to a cartoon-O of injustice and cries that pierce the ears. You are passed between arms and laps, cradled and crooned, distracted and calmed.

And now you nestle in arms that are made for this. We two comfortable people: you, small and calmed; I, cupping tiny feet in the palm of my hands. You turn your gaze to mine and smile.

The first time I met Louis, tears sprang to my eyes, a combination of tightened throat and hollowed heart. I wept for what I hadn't got and for the body that makes it difficult to attain.

I have no child, yet I am felled by exhaustion and malaise, and the unpredictability of relapse. Mine is an illness exacerbated by noise, by intense activity and sustained exertion, and my arms are empty still. How could I switch parenthood on and off as illness demands? Long hours in bed, too ill to read or write or talk, make time for thought. The images of Louis are lodged in my mind. I want to watch a baby of my own grow from infancy to childhood, into teen age and on to adulthood.

I make fictitious bargains: for a child I will risk this and this and this. In return for the cooperation of my body I will trade its range. But I have limits – aspects of

39

illness, of life, that are an exchange too far. I battle the fear of knowing how bad things can be and I battle the fear of knowing nothing at all.

Elbowing past the impossibility of flesh and blood, through a quagmire of can I and could I, and how, my resolve progresses and regresses and I move forward. I will use my body – *this* body. I will watch it work, discovering its possibilities, in awe of its results.

I hold in my mind the warmth and the breath of Louis, my arms encircling him. In the small hours, conviction finds me. There is a way to make this happen. I shall be a wonderful mother and, in a rejection of all caution, I will tear down hurdles and broadside the judgements of others. I will block all the murmurs of how hard, how easy, how irresponsible and just how. With these arms, that are waiting and in an absence of solutions I shall dream a remedy of my own.

My child will have Borrowed Parents. I can pick up the phone and they will leap into the breach. I will find the courage to ask for help. There in crisis, but with an involvement that stretches wider, these Borrowed Parents are more than parental friends, hangers-on, adoptive aunties or uncles. I trust them with the life and welfare of my own child. Wanting a child in their lives, they will make a friend of mine and my child's friendship is their reciprocation. They will take time to know my child, and me, to grasp our priorities and our desires and work with them. And, from somewhere, I will find within me the generosity to share.

Through them, my child catches the latest movie and plays in the park, there is a hand to hold at the dentist, a listener on the journey home from school. For when I am *too* ill, beyond the day-by-day of ill, my child's Borrowed Parents are my silence. They are my peace, my time for restoration where rest and sleep keep illness at bay. They make the quiet times in which I can be ill, a pause before I return to the haste of motherhood.

My child will live in a family extending far beyond nuclear notions. I take the seed of an idea from a friend and I make it my own. My child weaves through an infinity of relationships and guardians, a family that unfolds beyond boundaries. Parents and grandparents, friends and allies, mutuality with autonomy. Our family is extended, yet my child is my own.

I must find a way to transform dominating thought and habitual ache. I have reached an age, or perhaps a stage, and everywhere I am haunted by the motherhood of others. And my arms are open, waiting.

Part II
Setting Out

Somewhere a Mockingbird

Deborah Kent

When I was only a few weeks old my mother realized that I couldn't see. For the next eight months she and my father went from doctor to doctor searching for answers. At last their quest led them to one of the leading eye specialists in New York City. He confirmed everything they had already heard by that time – my blindness was complete, irreversible, and of unknown origin. He also gave them some sound advice. They should stop taking me to doctors, give up looking for a cure. Instead they should help me lead the fullest life possible. Fortunately for me, his prescription matched their best instincts.

As I was growing up people called my parents 'wonderful'. They were praised for raising me 'like a normal child'. As far as I could tell, my parents were like most of the others in my neighborhood – sometimes wonderful and sometimes annoying. And from my point of view I wasn't *like* a normal child – I *was* normal. From the beginning I learned to deal with the world as a blind person. I didn't long for sight any more than I yearned for a pair of wings. Blindness presented occasional complications, but it seldom kept me from anything I wanted to do.

For me blindness was part of the background music that accompanied my life. I had been hearing it since I was born, and paid it little attention. But others had a way of cranking up the volume. Their discomfort, doubts and concerns often put blindness at the top of the program. Teachers offered to lighten my assignments; scout leaders discouraged me from going on field trips; boys shied away from asking me on dates. The message was clear. I knew that my parents ached for me when these situations arose. It hurt them to see me being prejudged and rejected. Yet they found it hard to do battle on my behalf. Though they shared my sense of injury, they also identified with the non-disabled people who sought to exclude me. 'You have to understand how other people see things,' my parents told me. 'They're trying their best. You need to be patient with them.' I struggled to show the doubters and detractors that they were wrong. Much of the time I felt that I was fighting alone.

Since one of my brothers is also blind, it seemed more than likely that my unknown eye condition had a genetic basis. I never thought much about it until my husband Dick and I began to talk about having a child. Certainly genetics was not our primary concern. We married late (I was 31, Dick 42) and were used to living unencumbered. Since we both worked as freelance writers, our income was erratic. We had to think about how we could shape our lives to make room for a child, whatever child that might be.

But somehow blindness crept into our discussions. I don't remember which of us brought up the topic first. But once it emerged, it had to be addressed. How would I feel if I passed my blindness to our son or daughter? What would it mean to Dick, and to our extended families? What would it be like for us to raise a blind child together? I premised my life on the conviction that blindness was a neutral characteristic. It created some inconveniences, such as not being able to read print or drive a car. I believed that things could not have turned out any better if I had been fully sighted, so if my child were blind I would try to ensure it had every chance to become a self-fulfilled, contributing member of society. Dick said he agreed with me completely. We were deciding whether or not to have a child. Its visual acuity was hardly the point.

Yet if we truly believed our own words, why were we discussing blindness at all? I sensed that Dick was trying hard to say the right thing, even to believe it in his heart. But he was more troubled than he wished me to know. Once when I asked him how he would feel if he learned that our child was blind, he replied, 'I'd be devastated at first, but I'd get over it.' It was not the answer I wanted to hear.

I was blind and I was the woman Dick chose to marry, to spend his life with for better or for worse. He accepted my blindness naturally and comfortably, as a piece of who I was. If he could accept blindness in me, why would it be devastating to him if our child were blind as well? 'You know why,' was all he could tell me. 'You've got to understand.'

What I understood was that Dick, like my parents, was the product of a society that views blindness, and all disability, as fundamentally undesirable. All his life he had been assailed by images of blind people who were helpless, useless, and unattractive; misfits in a sight-oriented world. I had managed to live down that image. Dick had discovered that I had something of value to offer. But I had failed to convince him that it is really okay to be blind.

I wanted our child to be welcomed without reservation. I wanted Dick to greet its birth with joy. I did not know if I could bear his devastation if our baby turned out to be blind like me.

It was too painful to explore the implications any further. Instead I plunged into a search for information. After all, we didn't even know the real cause of my blindness. We couldn't make a decision until we gathered the facts. Surely the field of ophthalmology had learned something new over the past three decades. A series of phone calls led me to a specialist at New York University Medical Center. I was assured that if anyone could answer my questions, he was the man.

So, on a sunny morning in October, Dick and I set out for New York to learn why I am blind.

As we packed the car he commented, 'It's going to be a long, nervous day.' I couldn't have agreed with him more.

Parking on the streets of Manhattan was as difficult as

Dick had feared it would be. The city engulfed us with its fumes and bustle and grinding noise. We didn't try to talk above the traffic. Really there was nothing new to say.

We had walked several blocks when I became dimly aware of a strange sound. It was remarkably like the song of a bird, the clear, warbling notes ringing out against the concrete walls around us. At first I assumed it was a recording turned full blast, or some mechanical toy worked by a child. But as we drew nearer Dick remarked, 'There's a crowd of people standing by a tree. They're all looking at something. Oh hey, there's a bird up there!'

I've been an avid birder most of my life, and the song was unmistakable. It was a mockingbird. The mockingbird thrives in fields and gardens. It gathers scraps and snippets from the songs of other birds and braids them into a pattern all its own. The mockingbird sings exuberantly from April to June, but by late summer it usually falls silent. Yet this one poured forth its song on East 32nd Street in mid October, out of place and out of season. It seemed utterly fearless and confident, staking a claim for itself in that inhospitable city landscape. It had something to say, and it was determined to be heard.

New Yorkers are used to almost anything, but the extraordinary song of this tiny creature brought them to a standstill. For a little while Dick and I stood on the pavement, listening and marveling. Then we pushed through the revolving door and into the antiseptic halls of the medical center.

I expected a battery of tests, maybe a referral to yet another expert. But the doctor dilated my pupils, gazed into my eyes, and announced, 'I'll tell you what you have, and I'm 100 per cent certain. You've got Leber's congenital amaurosis.' Leber's is a genetic condition, he explained, autosomal recessive in nature. Both of my parents carried the recessive gene, and each of their children had a one-in-four chance of inheriting the eye condition.

What were my chances of passing Leber's on to my own children, I asked. The doctor explained that I would inevitably give one recessive gene for Leber's to my child. But unless my partner happened to carry the same recessive gene, there was no possibility that our child would be affected. The chances that Dick would prove to be another carrier were slight.

The discussion could have ended with that simple exchange of information. But the doctor had more to say. 'You have a good life, don't you?' he asked. 'If you have a child with Leber's, it can have a good life too. Go home and have a dozen kids if you want to!' Even from a total stranger those were wonderful words.

The trip to New York cemented our decision to have a child. Dick and I left the city with a new certainty, a sense that we were ready for whatever came our way. Yet I knew Dick was comforted by the fact that Leber's is relatively rare and that probably he did not carry the recessive gene. I wished he didn't need that comfort.

Within the year we were parents-to-be. We awaited the birth of our child with all the eagerness, wonder and anxiety common to expectant parents. We seldom mentioned the possibility that our baby might be blind but I lived with the small unspoken fear that, if our child were blind, Dick would feel betrayed – by medical science, by fate, by me.

Dick had his doubts about coaching me through labor and viewing the birth. To support us both his sister came along to our Lamaze classes. She even stayed with us in the birthing room in case Dick should faint dead away. But nobody fainted. When our daughter Janna arrived, we greeted her with greater joy than I could have imagined. Her welcome was boundless and wholly unreserved.

My parents flew out to visit us when we brought Janna home from the hospital. Mom helped with the cooking and housecleaning and insisted that I get as much rest as I could. I spent every conscious moment nursing, rocking, diapering, and marveling at the extraordinary new being who had entered our lives. I was too happy and excited to feel exhaustion.

I wasn't worried about Janna's vision or anything else. But one day my mother confided that my father had told her, 'We've still got to find out if the baby's blind.' I was stunned by his concern, and by her unquestioning acceptance that it was justified. My parents raised all three of their children, including my blind brother and me, with sensitivity and unwavering love. In all of us they tried to nurture confidence, ambition, and self-respect. Yet they felt apprehensive about the prospect that their granddaughter might also be blind.

It was almost time for Mom and Dad to go home when Dick said to my mother, 'You've raised two blind children. What do you think – can this kid see or not?' My mother said she really couldn't be sure. Janna was barely a week old; it was too soon to tell. The day after my parents left, Dick found the answer on his own. As Janna lay in his arms, awake and alert, he moved his hand back and forth above her face. Distinctly he saw her turn her head to track the motion. She saw his hand. She followed it with her eyes.

'She can see!' Dick exulted. He rushed to the phone and called my parents with the news. I listened quietly to their celebrations. I don't know if anyone noticed that I had very little to say.

How do I myself feel about the fact that Janna can see? I am glad that her world is enriched by color as well as texture and sound. When she snaps a picture with her new camera or poses before the mirror in her favorite dress I draw pleasure from her delight. As her mother I want her to have every advantage, and I know that some aspects of her life are easier because she has sight.

Beyond that, I am glad Janna will never be dismissed as incompetent and unworthy simply because she is blind. I am grateful that she will not face the discrimination that threads its way through my life and the lives of most people with disabilities. But I know her vision will not spare her from heartbreak. She will still meet disappointment, rejection, and self-doubt, as all of us must.

But in recent years a new insight has gradually come to me. Yes, my own loved ones hold the unshakeable belief that blindness is and always will be a problem. Nevertheless these same people have made me welcome. Though they dread blindness as a fate to be avoided at almost any cost, they give me their trust and respect. I don't understand how they live without discomfort amid such contradictions. But I recognize that people can and do reach out, past centuries of prejudice and fear, to forge bonds of love. It is a truth to marvel at, a cause for hope and perhaps some small rejoicing. And somehow it reminds me of the mockingbird that sang so boldly in a place where no one thought it belonged, making a crowd of busy people stand still to listen.

Wonderful Whirlwind

Merry Cross

Two weeks after my positive pregnancy test I dreamt of a swollen belly with two little faces pressing out on either side of the navel. I'd learned that you should especially trust dreams when you are pregnant. But I'd had no early scans, and neither the doctor nor the midwife confirmed the idea of a duo. In addition to which, perhaps because my stomach muscles were iron hard after years of walking with crutches, I never grew particularly large.

Anyway, I consciously gave up on the idea that it might be twins and celebrated another piece of good luck, which was that my back had never been better. Me, who had to visit the osteopath every two weeks to keep trouble at bay! Joyce, my osteopath, laughed when I joked that the best strategy for keeping my back in shape might be permanent pregnancy...

Joyce was the most assured and reassuring of all the professionals I dealt with. Her support was brilliant and I needed it, especially as it had been confirmed two weeks before the birth that I was indeed carrying twins! Joyce even left an important conference to help me with the labour. Val, a Tanzanian friend, was there too. It was just as well that I had such good supporters because the labour turned out to be a 45-hour marathon. No sooner did I reach the hospital than my previously regular contractions went haywire. It was 18 hours before they came at regular 5-minute intervals. More hours passed until I was sufficiently dilated. More again as they tried to insert the needle to deliver the epidural into my whacky spine. Then the pushing started but, in spite of my strong muscles, it produced nothing. Eventually a doctor came in and announced, 'We'd like to help you but we've an

Date ___ 11/50 Copies ___ 1 ___ Reserve ___
Source ___ Trade X ___ Text ___ BIP ___ Other ___

Paperback ☒ Hardcover ☐ Other ☐

Author ___ Waters, Gwen Frostic

Title ___ Bigger Than the Sky: Disabled Women on Parenting

Publisher ___ Women's Pr Ltd. ___ 7153

ISBN ___ 0704 245455

Price (Estimated) ___ Ed ___ Vol ___ ©

Gen LM Dontuffee
emailed pub at JoC the Women's press.
$20 cm.

Deposit DPO Rush ___ Pending ___ Clerk ___

Form # 59117

HSS: (530) 752-3369

UCD BOOKSTORE bune order
Sept 18th.
University of California
Davis, CA 95616
Main Store: (530) 752-2944
UCDMC: (916) 734-3452

Office of Admin.
(Adams)
Atn it Admin.

Department (if billed to DPO) ___

Name ___

Address ___ Office Admin.
City ___ State ___ Zip ___

Daytime Phone ___ 2-3372

E-mail address ___

☐ Pickup   DPO# ___
☐ Mail   ID ___
☒ Campus Mail TAG ___

D6248 (7/99)M

Date _____ Copies 1 _____ Reserve _____
Sou̲r̲c̲e̲ Trade X̲ Text _____ BIP _____ Other _____

Paperback ☐ Hardcover ☐ Other ☐

Author _____
Title _____ 7153
Publisher _____ 704 245455
ISBN _____
Price (Estimated) _____ Ed ____ Vol. ____ © ____

_____ LM Renrure
_____ e-mailed pub at _____

Deposit _____ Rush _____ Pending _____ Clerk _____

UCD BOOKSTORE back order
Sept 18th.
University of California
Davis, CA 95616
Main Store: (530) 752-2944
UCDMC: (916) 734-3452

Form #
59117
HSS: (530) 752-3369

Office of Admin.
(Adams)

Department (if billed to DPO) _____
Name _____
Address _____
City _____ State ____ Zip ____
Daytime Phone _____ 2-7775
E-mail address _____

☐ Pickup   DPO# _____
☐ Mail   ID _____
☐ Campus Mail   TAG _____

D6248 (7/99)M

UCD BOOKSTORE
University of California, Davis
Davis, CA 95616

Deliver to:

YOUR SPECIAL ORDER HAS ARRIVED

emergency caesarean to attend. Try to stop pushing for an hour or so.'

If you think pushing is hard, try *not* pushing... I tried, I really tried, but when the doctor returned and repeated the same advice an hour later, Val said calmly, in Kiswahili so as not to spark a fight with the attendant midwife, 'Merry, you've borne these children for nine months – just push. You can do it.' I did and my first-born began to show her head and was eventually helped out with a suction cap. Her sister went for a little walkabout in her newly spacious home and then took the plunge, arriving five minutes later.

At only 3lb 4oz, my second-born daughter was whisked off to an incubator and stayed there for a week or so until all the necessary interventions were over and I had persuaded staff that she would put on weight more quickly in the company of her mother and sister. Meanwhile I'd been trying to accustom staff to the idea that disabled women *do* have babies and need access to facilities such as baths. I was told, 'We've never had a disabled mother here before.' It was all too easy to believe, given their total lack of preparedness for such an eventuality. But I have to admit it puzzled me, seasoned campaigner that I am, that I hadn't discussed my needs fully with the maternity department before the event. I think the rosy glow of pregnancy must have got the better of my brain!

We were destined to be stuck in hospital for three weeks whilst the local social services department ground slowly into action to sort out a care package for me. But in truth, I was lucky again. The girls had timed their arrival to perfection, entering the world only weeks after the enactment of the so-called Care in the Community Act. The combination of this act with the very recent Children Act meant that the local authority was still trying to show how well it could comply with the new legislation and in addition was still flush enough to fund the 24-hour help I needed as a single mother. Still, I doubt I would have got it without the intervention of my first advocate, Jenny, herself a disabled mother. She had the assertiveness and bluntness that, at that point, I lacked. Strange how we can advocate for others but go to pieces when it's our own welfare that's at stake!

After a visit by the agency supervisor during which some of the questions I was asked seemed to me outrageous and unnecessary, my first helper finally appeared. A Nigerian woman called Vicky, she instantly fell in love with the children and stayed with us most nights until the girls were about 15 months old. She was the first of many lovely women from around the world to enter our lives. For the first six weeks at home, agency support was augmented by the presence of my wonderful friend and baby addict, Bharti, who took it upon herself to help in every way she could. Bharti helped to ensure that my milk production was rarely at a standstill, despite me having two little mouths to feed, by keeping up a constant flow of the most delicious food. Bharti, Vicky and I were kept pretty busy and it was with growing alarm that I contemplated my friend's departure at the end of the six weeks.

Within a very short space of time I had gone from living alone to living with two small girls and one or other of a changing team of international helpers. At the time I was desperately grateful that help had been made available. The few disastrous appointments were despatched promptly back to the agency. But gradually I became concerned about several child protection issues.

For example, although these agencies are supposed to do police checks before sending staff to work with children, it was clear that they did not. Some of my workers walked into the agency one day and were on the job the next, whilst police checks take weeks to complete. I was asking my children to accept a large number of strangers having very close contact with them. At first they didn't seem to mind, but over time it became clear that they did, so I performed all the intimate tasks myself until the girls had got to know and relax with a new worker. But it was inevitable, with twins especially, that they would sometimes be in the care of someone else when I was not in the room and, very occasionally, when I was not in the house. I found making decisions about the extent to which I trusted people very difficult at times.

The process of getting to know and relate to helpers, teaching them how I wanted them to deal with the girls, learning from them, feeling dependent on them and then losing them (usually to better paid jobs) was stressful. Still I am happy that my daughters started life knowing people of so many races and cultures and that their own richly diverse band of friends reflects their feeling at ease with anyone, so long as they are good fun.

As budgets began to dwindle, my relationship with social services became strained. They could not understand that the girls' eczema (which developed around the time of their first vaccinations) demanded literally hours of extra care; additional shopping, cooking and bathing. 'Care Managers' came and went and at the worst point I was informed by a social worker and her line manager that whilst the Children and Families Team thought it was a matter for the Adult Disability Team, the latter thought the reverse, so that in the end it was possible that neither of them would fund my care package. Once again the support of an advocate proved crucial and we were able to persuade the Adult Team that it was their responsibility to facilitate me as a parent.

I do remember peaceful moments, especially before I went back to work and whilst the girls were young enough to need substantial sleeps during the day. These moments got fewer with the girls' increasing mobility, but if I lacked peace I didn't lack entertainment. In fact, it's the fun I hadn't bargained for. I knew it would be hard work and in all fairness it *is* hard, but it didn't occur to me that there would be so much sheer enjoyment. My greatest joy is the first minutes of each morning, playing with the girls in bed. I can recall all the different phases of the games we have played, which, even though they have become more and more rough and tumble as time goes by, I can still largely cope with when I'm on my back.

Perhaps one reason I love those early morning moments of play is because they are so unpressurised. Generally, getting myself and two little people out of the house has meant whirling between changing bags, feeding bottles, clothes, potties, toilets and, more recently, preparing meals that don't contain allergens to take to nursery.

I am lucky in having relatively calm children who spend more time entertaining each other than fighting and who have phenomenal attention spans and powers of concentration. Nevertheless, the impact of requests, coming at high speed, in stereo and with great assertiveness, can send my brain into a spin. Still, if there is any spin or whirlwind I have to be in, then let it be this one.

Gonzilla the Ape Woman Gets Angry

Jill Daly

I feel his moist, soft breath on my cheek as he slips his hand under my hair, caressing the small of my neck. My mother warned me about boys like this. With his eyes half closed, his mouth a fraction from mine I realise, too late, what he is up to. The pain is sudden and intense.

'Let go, let go of Mummy's nose.'

No longer a baby, he is a shark.

My voice becomes desperate.

'Let go, let go, you're hurting mummy.'

Keir starts to giggle, loosens the grip on my nose and tries to stand on his head. My mother was right about boys like this: so unpredictable.

Keir is two years and one week old. He has just realised that whereas most people have two arms, mummy only has one. He thinks I am terribly clever to be like this. I am reminded of my eight-year-old nephew who, when explaining to his class that his aunt was disabled and only had one arm, heard a small voice pipe up from the back row, 'Huh! That's nothing. My mum's got *no* arms.'

My ticket to the wacky world of disabled people came quite unexpectedly, courtesy of a bus driver who thought it perfectly reasonable to drive a bus forward whilst looking backwards. I was 29. Strangely I had always felt sorry for the driver, as it must have been quite a shock to run someone over. I say 'had' because all those benevolent feelings changed when Keir arrived on the scene.

As a newly disabled person I was shocked to discover that I couldn't rely on certain things as I had done in my previous non-disabled incarnation. Even while I was in hospital medical staff were advising me not to have children. A nurse took Mac (my partner who became my

57

husband a year later) aside and whispered,

'Leave her if you want to. She's disabled. Don't stay with her just because you feel you ought to.'

Once out of hospital I realised that these assumptions and prejudices were commonplace and that disabled people had been subject to them for centuries.

What could I do but join the struggle? I gave up teaching (well, okay, they made me redundant), joined a local disability rights group, and became an equal opportunities officer in local government.

Time was passing. Mac and I had been married for three years and decided that we wanted to start a family.

To be euphemistic, we tried. We tried an an awful lot. Nothing happened.

In 1993 I was informed by a nurse who must have completed her training under the dragon-like matron from the *Carry On* series that I didn't stand a chance of having a baby because I was polycystic. 'Polycystic women,' boomed the nurse, so that everyone in the fertility clinic could hear, 'are fat, spotty and have lots of superfluous hair.' My God, not only was I disabled and infertile, I was now about to turn into Gonzilla the ape woman. The fact that I was thin and past the acne stage (well, almost) didn't seem to bother her. She hadn't finished. 'Not only do you not ovulate,' she graciously added, 'but you kill off your husband's sperm. You have hostile mucous.' Blimey, now I sounded like an extra from *Star Wars*.

A consultant informed me that I would need to consider fertility drugs and in vitro fertilisation even to be in with a chance of becoming pregnant. After the shock, the weight of depression descended.

Realising that I was infertile was a shock to my system in a way that becoming disabled never was. Nothing seemed worth the effort. Life became a string of pointless exercises. I had never realised just how much having children meant to me. Perhaps none of us ever does until the day we realise we can't.

And then out of the darkness – light. Mac and I were beginning to realise that although we wanted children they didn't need to be our birth children. At the beginning of 1994 we embarked upon an adoption course with our local authority with the hope of adopting a sibling group of two or three children above the age of three.

Having encountered discrimination in various forms I wondered whether my impairment would go against the adoption. We hear so often from the media that adopting children is practically impossible and that prospective parents seem to be turned down on the slightest whim. What we are not told is that there are many, many toddlers and children waiting to be adopted in this country. It's just that some people will insist on new-born, 'perfect' babies – in other words, non-disabled sheets of (supposedly) blank paper. So, imagine my joy when my impairment was seen as a positive quality. Our social workers reckoned that, having had to put up with people's prejudices on a daily basis, I would be better placed to empathise with the children who were also in that position.

There was one point in the adoption process, however, which did annoy us. Near the beginning of the course we had to say which impairments we were 'prepared to accept'. It basically came down to box ticking: Would you take a child with cerebral palsy? Would you take a child with a visual impairment? The list went on and on. We refused to play ball, stating that we would consider the children first and then any impairment, but not the other way round. This proved to be quite a problem for the social workers, but eventually they accepted our decision and our comments were passed on.

Finally the day came when we were presented with our completed papers. Now all we needed to do was wait for the 'panel' day when our application would either be approved or turned down by a panel of social workers and members of the public. The time couldn't pass quickly enough. We were both on tenterhooks. I missed a period. I assumed this was stress. A friend advised me to do a pregnancy test. I told her not to be so ridiculous. I did a test. It was positive.

Very few people understood how we felt. It was assumed that we must be over the moon.

'How wonderful!' was the general consensus. 'Now you will have a child of your own.'

Why do some people see adopted children as second best, as not being your 'own'? Do genes and DNA make so much difference? If I am truthful, during the first months of my pregnancy I did not want to be pregnant. I was confused and upset. Although we had not got as far as being matched with any children I was grieving for them all the same. It was not until the third month when my GP mistakenly believed that I was miscarrying, that the child inside me suddenly became a reality and I realised how much I wanted it.

I refused all ante-natal screening. One doctor, who assumed my impairment was congenital, urged me to have the tests. There seems to be a general assumption in the medical establishment that disabled parents do not want to have disabled children. Perhaps it goes hand in hand with the myth that we are all sitting around waiting for a cure.

And then the worries started about how I would cope looking after a baby. Adopting children who are past infancy is one thing; looking after a baby another.

I reassured everyone. I even reassured myself.

Shortly after I became disabled an American woman, with the same impairment as myself; had introduced herself to me. She has been an amazing role model – a one-time lawyer and a mother of three children. She made having and caring for babies seem as easy as falling off a log. So, naturally, I couldn't wait to prove to everyone how simple it would be for me. Perhaps I should also add that I was not unused to childcare, having worked as an au pair for six different families during my twenties.

Our son, Keir, was born on 17 June 1995. Right from the start nothing went as I had imagined. As soon as Keir was born I put him to my breast only to be greeted by a look which said, 'What in God's name am I supposed to do with that?' So much for the natural rooting reflex. Oddly, I didn't get worked up about this, as I had read somewhere that following earthquakes new-born babies are pulled out alive for up to 14 days. Positioning Keir was difficult. I have a vague memory of almost standing on my head on the bed at one point. In the end I gave up and relied on the nurses running to help whenever I rang the bell.

'But how will you cope when you go home?' people asked.

I didn't really want to think about it and, besides, the puddings were really good. I have a weakness for traditional British puds. I ended up staying a week.

Whilst in hospital adaptations were made for me. I couldn't cope with the standard hospital 'cot', so I was given one with lower sides. I was moved to a side room. I was never quite sure whether this was more for the other patients' benefit or mine. I had noticed a few visiting partners or husbands staring when they caught sight of my stump. Whatever the reason, the move was bliss. There's nothing like having your own loo after giving birth.

One day stays in my mind. Three nurses came in and asked whether I 'had a social worker'. I froze. Two weeks before I had Keir I had listened to a documentary on Radio Four in which three disabled mothers talked about how their children had been forcibly taken into care. I stonily replied that the only social workers I knew were friends and that I would have plenty of help from my family. This latter remark was a blatant lie. My husband's family live 300 miles away and my mother was recovering from cancer. I realise now that these nurses really did want to get some help for me. And I threw their offer back in their faces.

The honeymoon period was over. Mac and I returned

home with our week-old son. For a while I seemed to have endless energy – probably due to all those puddings I'd consumed in hospital – but then everything started to work against me. I now know that this is an extremely difficult time for any new mother but I began to think, in my exhausted state, that it was just me.

We discovered that there was no child car seat on the British market that I could use. It took me half an hour to change Keir's nappy; it took even longer to change his clothes. I couldn't do the safety straps up on his pushchair. I was too exhausted to cook so we lived on take-aways which made me ill. I seemed to be sinking, losing control.

I think that it was around this time that Mac told me that he had never really considered me a disabled person until he saw me struggling every day with Keir. I was shocked into speechlessness. Mac informed me that he was trying to come to terms with the situation. As it seemed to me then – this meant spending more time at work and less at home. I felt as though I were fighting a war on my own. Of course, with hindsight, I realise that many, many couples go through an extremely difficult time a few months after the first child is born. So much for a baby cementing a relationship!

So I developed strategies. I went for the easiest route every time. As the breastfeeding was now going well, I did not introduce him to solids until he was eight months old. I sought out the old style babygros with just three or four buttons down the front. Keir lived in these, day and night, for sometimes as much as a week at a time. I abandoned my principles and switched from 'green' terry nappies to modern disposables. As I couldn't get him into a car seat I gave up using the car and went everywhere on foot with the pushchair. I swallowed my pride and contacted social services. I had wanted someone to help me in the home with Keir for a few hours a week. This was not possible, but they could offer me two sessions a week with a local childminder to allow me space to get on with those wonderful, womanly occupations such as shopping and cleaning. I eventually accepted.

And then, just when I thought I was coping, disaster struck. When Keir was 18 months old I developed repetitive strain injury in my remaining arm. The pain was intense: I couldn't lift a toothbrush let alone my son. I couldn't push the pushchair.

We had to find a nursery for Keir.

I was heartbroken. Having looked after children some years previously I had always vowed that I would look after my own children myself. I was discovering that it was easier to be a working disabled mother than a disabled mother who stays at home. The irony of the situation hurt me intensely.

I became angry, I began to hate myself. For the first time, I didn't want to be disabled. I wanted my arms back. I wanted to have my baby with me all the time. I didn't want to see his little pale face in tears as he was left at the nursery or with the childminder. He was in pain. I was in pain. I hated the bus driver who knocked me down and changed my life. I wanted to seek him out and shout:

'Look! See what you have done! I love my little boy, I want to keep him at home and look after him myself, but instead I have to send him to strangers.'

I wanted to find out his address, turn up on his doorstep and then hit him over the head with a mallet.

I had flashbacks of the courses I used to run in which I strove to correct the image that disabled people are all angry, bitter people. And now here was I, Gonzilla the ape woman, gone totally and utterly berserk.

Panic Attack

Linda M Gordon

Seated on my bed, sweat-dampened sheets thrown back, I try to slow my breathing. It's 3 a.m., and fear sits heavily like a great beast on my chest, choking out air and reason. Tidal waves of heat surge up under my rib cage and roll over my belly and thighs, leaving rivulets of sweat in their wake. Drawing in a slow, measured breath, I fight the feeling of tumbling over backwards into blackness. *Is this what dying is like*, my racing mind wonders.

It's not the first time that this thought has come, unbidden, with the panic that hauls me up so roughly from sleep. Shards of a broken nightmare leave me bleeding fear; I'm breathless, rabbit-hearted. Some quiet corner of my mind, the part that knows that I'm okay, really, struggles to assert itself and fails.

How many times in how many years have I burst forth from sleep, hurling myself blindly at the telephone in a primal cry for help? Clutching the white receiver tightly in my hand, fighting the dizziness that threatens to envelop me, I dial 9-1-1. Holding my breath, I endure an eternity before the dispatcher answers on the second ring. Rapidly, I run down my address and my symptoms. My name is always an afterthought.

Recognizing my voice, the dispatcher's tone changes from urgent to impatient. *We've played this game before*, the edge in her voice seems to say. Sighing deeply, she tells me the unit is on its way. *A waste of time!* The unspoken words seem to travel through the telephone line as clearly as if she had shouted them. 'Thank you,' I breathe.

Quickly, I dial my mother. The conversation is terse and predictable, and I hear the strain in her voice as she promises to be here soon. Hanging up the receiver, I wait.

This waiting is the hardest part. Hanging my head, I don't notice the riot of coral and periwinkle cosmos on the beige field of my nightgowned lap. I am seeing in my mind, a collage of other early morning calls that punctuate the last 15 years of my life. Each one I vowed would be the last. I can't believe that I've come to this terror-filled place again. Soon, I become conscious of wet spots blooming among the flowers in my lap. Holding out my hands, I catch the teardrops like rain on my palms.

Hearing the commotion of ambulance and squad car in the driveway, I lift my head to see my son standing silently in the doorway. Blue cotton pajamas hang from his slight frame, as he holds his shoulders rigidly. His huge brown eyes seem larger still in a face gone white with worry. His jaw is set, and his thin arms are pulled taut across his chest as he hugs himself tightly.

'Jeff,' I call softly and hold out my arms. He flows quickly into them and is swallowed up in my love and my regret. 'I love you.'

I can feel his head nodding against my breast. He knows. *Will that love be enough to make up for these interrupted nights*, I question silently. *And will you be able to forgive your growing up too fast?*

'My medication isn't working, Jeff,' I explain slowly through my tears. Another nod. This is well-traveled ground we're covering now. 'I'm going to have to go to the emergency room, but I'll be okay. Meme will be here soon.'

'I know, Mom,' he says tightly, too brave for his nine years.

The paramedics have opened the front door and are calling out to me as I kiss Jeff's softly rounded cheek.

'I'm here.'

Holding Jeff close for just a moment longer, I breathe in the warm, citrus scent that rises from his tousled hair. Then I let him go and walk out the front door, missing him already.

Jamie and Me

Janet Pedley

My name is Janet. I live in my own flat. I did not know I was pregnant till I was five months gone. In June I had a little boy called Jamie Lee, he was born on 7.6.89. When I came out of hospital I went to stay with some people who would look after me and the baby. They were called Vivienne and Dave. I stayed with them for three months. I went back to my own flat where I looked after the baby. At the age of six months he went into care – he went to stay with my sister and brother-in-law because I could not look after him. I see him every weekend. My sister does things for him. I could do things for him. He knows I am his mummy and my sister is auntie. He will be nine years old in June. I hope one day that me and Jamie will be back together again. When Jamie grows up he will be old enough to come and see me at my flat.

A Damned Good Job

Ellen Basani

The summer afternoon was Mediterranean hot. Being pregnant, I felt perfectly entitled to do nothing but lie around, resting and warming my limbs. After all I had another life to consider. Reluctantly I roused myself to answer the phone. 'Ellen, hello, it's Judy.' What could my doctor be wanting on a Saturday afternoon? 'I don't want to worry you but your blood test has come back, and things are not quite right.' Panic, pure and deadly, lunged at my peace and won. Judy was saying something about an appointment on Monday at nine, with the haematologist. 'Yes, I understand Judy, yes Monday morning, yes I'll be there.' I went on nodding at the blank wall in front of me, barely taking in the details. In her determinedly calm voice, I sensed deep concern. Something was terribly wrong. Doctors don't ring patients on weekends just to impart routine blood results. 'Probably nothing serious, but better get it checked out,' the precise and kindly voice continued.

'You thought you could escape,' mocked something savage within my brain. 'You're not meant to have a child.' On and on it mocked. My husband, bewildered by my terror, tried to bring back some reality into my unfocused thinking, but his own anxiety caused him to retreat. It was with bleak determination that I walked towards the haematologist's. As she told me of the dramatic loss of platelets and its implications, I listened, not really surprised. Hadn't I always known I was not meant to live a 'normal' life?

Forty years ago, in a small country town in Australia, I was enrolled at the local Catholic school. Fearing my exclusion, my parents neglected to inform the Head Teacher of my severe visual impairment. The Ozzie identity in fifties Australia was strongly connected to physical prowess, independence and the pioneer spirit. 'Being handicapped' frequently consigned children like me to an enclosed life at home, or to exile in the large institutions of the city. Parents were left to bear their fear and grief alone.

It took my teacher nine months to realise I couldn't see and I became extremely skilled at passing. The odd thing was that nothing changed once my impairment was discovered. No special help was forthcoming. The result was inevitable. By the end of primary education I was coming last in class and, added to the shame of being different, came the constant humiliation of those tell-tale school reports, which were distributed publicly by the Head Nun. Unable to attribute this failure to its social cause, I blamed myself. To an eight-year-old the reason was obvious – I was stupid.

Social isolation in an environment where everyone else had vision became so acute, that all break times were spent unoccupied and friendless. Faces and play-ground activities were just a blur. The nuns seemed to be unable to help the children understand my different needs because of their own discomfort. Their way of dealing with those difficulties was to ignore them.

So, seeing myself as stupid and unworthy of friends, I would flee to the chapel where I could at least be with someone who loved me – God! He became my all: father, friend and guide. No one else was entrusted with my private grief and I was prepared to forsake anything to maintain this union with Him. I was fertile ground for distorted messages. Those same nuns who had ignored my practical needs, suggested my 'handicap' made me special in God's eyes. One of the few who were chosen. Nowhere else was I special. Such messages were balm to a lacerated ego. I was told that I had been singled out by my Adored Father to carry a Cross just like the Blessed Saviour. His mother Mary was also chosen and she offered complete surrender to the will of God. How could I offer anything less?

To me complete surrender meant living the life of a holy ascetic, with eyes fixed longingly on the next world and even deeper, blissful union with the Almighty. There was no higher calling, or so the nuns would have me believe. This meant casting off any prospect of knowing the worldly pleasures of marriage and children – small sacrifice to a child desperate to retain her exalted status. So I held fast to my sense of ennobled destiny, despite adolescent distractions. Then came young womanhood, and the agony of falling in love.

I was 26, holding down a responsible, professional job, when into my life bounced a man who seemed to love me. The childhood feelings of exclusion and invisibility were temporarily quenched. He was charmed. I was overjoyed. But there it was, the old message which I had tried to forget. My life was meant to be consecrated to the will of God, not to love and marriage. The tussle was between the waiting God and me. I broke under the strain and the man went away.

Eight years later I had recovered enough from the round of guilt and fear to marry without excessive anxiety. But finding out that I was pregnant reopened the old scars. From the moment my GP called, events began to spiral downwards. Looking back, each successive trauma seemed to shout 'Retribution!'

'Low platelets', I was told, 'could be a symptom of leukaemia.' Even I had not thought of this possibility. A deeply invasive bone marrow test ruled this out, but the platelets continued to fall away and I was still in danger of haemorrhaging. The full force of the NHS took me over like a powerless rag doll, with constant blood tests, high doses of steroids and, for the last two weeks, a daily platelet transfusion lasting eight hours.

My waters broke in a slow leak and I was admitted to

hospital early and induced to reduce the threat of infection. The acupuncturist, basket of calming essential oils and soothing new age music tape were swept away under the full weight of a high-tech birth.

Labour and delivery were even more terrifying than I had imagined. It lasted 24 hours, the contractions came very rapidly and the baby became caught in the birth canal. Thankfully, the innate will to survive overwhelmed the jumble of irrational thinking. Amazingly my heart did not stop beating, nor did my child's. Maybe it was his strong, rapid heartbeat on the monitor that kept me going.

When my baby was given to me and my fingers traced dully over his perfectly formed body, they came to rest on his head. Horrified, my hands recoiled. The forehead, which I had expected to be smooth and well rounded, felt jagged and deformed. Could I have given birth to a monster after all I'd been through? No one else seemed bothered. The nurses saw to tidying up and my husband was crooning with delight at his beautiful boy. Why didn't they notice his zigzag, misshapen forehead? This was the last straw. All those months of terror, culminating in a traumatic high risk birth, and now this. This I could not endure. God had won after all. Passing the baby over to his doting dad, I fled into the deepest, darkest hole in my psyche. My body was still there being sewed and washed, but I felt no love for the baby I had just struggled to give life to. How could I love in another human being that which I most feared and rejected in myself – physical imperfection?

It took two days before guilt seared me back to face reality. Because my mother had recoiled from her blind baby, I had always felt devoid of a centre. Through my actions, history was repeating itself: I was abandoning my child. The unwillingness to wound another human as I had been wounded propelled me to have my baby returned from the nursery.

Alone with the child, my child, I gingerly felt his head.

Of course, the bones had settled. The surge of relief, joy and intense love flooded into the deep hollow that had yawned open at his birth. I cradled him, crooning and caressing, like any new mother, and knew bliss for the first time in my life. We had survived.

His feeding I saw to but not his personal care. I felt overwhelmed by the enormity of caring for this new-born baby, just like any other new mother. So I let the nurses bathe him and change his nappy, while I hid behind my visual impairment.

On the third night, after I had requested to have my baby sleep with me, his little body began to make staccato movements. I asked my midwife if babies always made funny, twitchy movements. Reassured by her relaxed response, I went on enjoying him. When the twitching happened again the next morning, I asked to see the paediatrician with only a passing shaft of anxiety. He came and examined my healthy-looking boy and pronounced him fine. 'Over anxious, can't see' was the likely response as he made his way to the door.

Suddenly my beautiful, healthy boy began to shake again. The paediatrician saw and responded immediately. Within half an hour I was alone in my hospital bed. The cot containing my son was on its way to intensive care. All I could do was wait, wild eyed and very much alone.

Ten o'clock that night, in they trooped. Three paediatricians and a hoard of others, probably nurses, maybe even the porter. Only the doctors were introduced. How I got through that interview I will never know. My baby was critically ill. My beautiful, newly found beloved child, I was told, might not last the night. He was fitting badly and they suspected meningitis. I began to rock with horror.

With the intervention of a concerned paediatric consultant and very strong drugs, I found oblivion that night. My presence in intensive care seemed not to be welcomed, as the staff fought for my baby's life. Years of believing that sighted people knew best, especially sighted medical staff, allowed my passivity to keep me from his bedside. Their authority had replaced that of the Almighty. Whatever feeble protest I made was gently but firmly discounted. My husband, unable to bear any of it, had left the hospital in a daze. This lack of emotional support was familiar to me, and so I sought nothing better.

My boy did survive and thus began three weeks of very slow recovery. In those days I was allowed to stay in hospital with him. At home, because of my husband's learning difficulties and my own passivity, little was structured or accessible. Simply making a cup of tea was an ordeal; preparing meals was a minefield. My mother's first words began to take on more resonance: 'How are you going to cope with a new baby?' The more I relinquished my caring role to the staff, the more I blocked out the reality of having to manage alone at home.

But five days before discharge my baby was released from special care back onto the ward. The time had come for me to bath the scrap of humanity entrusted to my care. Every eye felt riveted to my back as I trundled the cot towards the washing facilities. Like any other new mother, the first experience of bathing a squirming little body was terrifying. Fear diminished with practice however. 'Fancy that!' spectators would whisper, as I successfully performed the simplest of tasks.

Two days before discharge, another woman dressed my little boy in his first street clothes and escorted him to another hospital for a brain scan. The woman I am now can't believe that the earlier me did not stamp my feet and demand to accompany him. I pleaded and was gently but firmly refused. All I felt able to do was cry and entreat the ambulance driver to please go carefully.

To experience my baby being carried away by another woman broke something in me. Finally, I became angry. I was no longer a child to be discounted, nor a receptacle for uncomfortable feelings about disability. That was my baby being driven away. It was MY place to be with him, like it had been my place to be in intensive care. No more would

I apologise for my existence. I had exercised my right, just like any other woman, to produce a child. Neither God nor society had the right to take my mothering role from me. I vowed there in my hospital room, while awaiting the return of that precious child, that I would allow nothing, no one to disempower me again.

My boy is 11 now. He has an amazing, powerful, young sister. I am attempting to raise them outside the unsupportive marriage. The God of old, the yearning for acceptance, has been supplanted by deep inner love. My children are strong, compassionate individuals who don't fear difference. My mothering is a cause for celebration. Despite the limited support, I am doing a damned good job!

Me, I am a Mother

Sue Norris

Birth
Joy amongst the pain;
I give
birth to new life.

I Am a Mother
Me,
I am a mother.
It has been an experience.
I tried to get the right help
to give my son the best.
It did not happen,
so we did everything together
and left the rest
we could not do.
It was ingenious,
what I thought up.
I did it for the best.
If I'd asked for help,
no one would have done anything,
only laughed in my face for trying.

My Child
I hit him.
Why?

I needed help;
but no one noticed;
nothing happened;
still,
life goes on.

I hit him.
He
did not get help;
he got left,
my child.

My Son
To know
my son's out there,
I don't know where
he is
I just remember
what fun we had
when we knew each other.

A Boy
A boy sat opposite me
on the bus.
It could have been you.
I saw him with the corner of my eye,
his aura met mine.
But the boy did not know
I watched him.
In the way he showed himself to me
He reminded me of you,
In all your splendour.

I thought I could send a message
through him to you.

My Boy
Ah, my boy,
the one left long ago at the station,
I pass where I left you.
Now you are grown.
Who are you?
How do you look?
I do not know.
I wish I did.

In My Mind's Eye: II
Pregnancy and birth

Jo Litwinowicz

On New Year's Day I went into hospital for what I thought would be a fortnight but I ended up staying there until my child was born, four months later. The consultant told me I had very high blood pressure and said he would like to keep me in hospital for at least a fortnight so they could run some tests. He assured me that there was nothing to worry about as far as the baby was concerned. Instead of rising, my weight had fallen. I was usually nine stone but now I weighed seven and a half. Every time I ate or drank I got terrible indigestion and had to be sick, and every so often I used to feel dizzy.

Even though I'd spent half my life in hospital I felt very nervous this time. The nursing staff weren't at ease handling me at first. I don't think there was much call for helping a severely disabled mum through her pregnancy. I was put in a room on my own. Because I was on a drip and they could only use my good hand for it, I couldn't even read a book. I didn't have a television to lessen the boredom and there wasn't anyone to talk to. The nurses were walking round me as if they were treading on eggshells and I was too frightened to say anything in case it upset the running of the ward. The bed was too high for me to get out of, so I had to use a bedpan, which I hated. I couldn't even look forward to visiting hours because it was impossible for my husband to come during the week. He worked till 5.30 p.m. and the last bus home again was at 6 p.m. On Sunday the last bus was at 2 p.m. This meant I could only see my husband once a week, on Saturdays, but we wrote to each other twice a week and it was like courting all over again!

On the fifth day they found a lower bed for me and I was put on the main ward. I soon settled down, the other women got used to me and we chatted endlessly. At the end of the fortnight the consultant said he thought it would be better if I stayed with them till my baby was born so that they could monitor us carefully. I knew I would be in the best place if anything went wrong, and I was grateful to them for caring, but I regretted not being able to share this important time with my husband, preparing for the birth of our baby, him missing the first kick and the bonding of the three of us. So every Saturday the nurses made my husband's visit very special and important. They waited for my husband to come before they put the monitor on me to see and hear the baby's heartbeat and I had scans when he was there.

On Monday mornings the consultant and his students always ended up round my bed discussing how my baby was going to be born, as I wanted a natural birth. I didn't want to be put to sleep and miss the big moment. So every week we used to talk about how we were going to do it so as to minimise my spasms.

From about seven and a half months the consultant was getting worried about me and kept saying they should start thinking about inducing the baby but I kept prolonging it by saying I was okay. But as April came he put his foot down and it was decided that the great day was going to be 24 April and that I would be awake for it, so I was over the moon.

At 9 p.m. on Easter Sunday, I had a bath while the nurse prepared the woman opposite me, as they were going to induce her. We were laughing and she kept saying, 'You wait, it will be your turn in about ten days and I'm coming back to torment you when you deliver.' So I said, 'Like Dick Turpin saying, "Stand and Deliver",' and we all roared with laughter. Even the nurses joined in after a bit. At 10 a.m. I lay down and found I was wet, even though I had just been to the loo. I told the nurse and she said, 'It's all that laughing. I'll be with you when I finish.' By this time the mattress was absolutely sodden. I couldn't understand it as I was sure I hadn't drunk that much. When the nurse came she took one look and said, 'Your waters have broken, you're in labour.' I didn't know what to think, it was as if a hundred and one things went through my mind in that moment. The ward was cheering and the woman who was going to be induced said, 'It's not fair, I went through all that preparation for tomorrow and you go into labour!'

My consultant was away on holiday so his standby came to see me at 11 p.m.. He knew that I wanted to be awake but he said that this was very unexpected, they weren't at full staff and it was the middle of the night, so there was no alternative but to put me to sleep. I was disappointed but on the other hand I wanted the baby to arrive so I didn't mind. I was told they'd be ready for me about 2 a.m.. Meanwhile a nurse phoned my friend to see if my husband could come down.

My son was born on Easter Monday at 2.45 a.m. and weighed 6lb 6oz. The nurse brought him out for my husband to hold, so he was the first to see him. I would love to have seen my husband's face when he held the baby. I remember waking up in a ward with my husband standing by the bed and asking him what we had.

When I saw my son the tears streamed down my face; it was the greatest moment of my life. But after a while, when he was feeding, I suddenly had this strange sensation that I didn't have any maternal feeling towards him. I knew that I loved this baby but it wasn't real love, it was a weird feeling and I can't find the right words to express it. I didn't dare tell anyone how I was feeling, in case they took my son away. I didn't even tell my husband, and so it just stayed bottled inside me.

At 9 a.m. the ward sister asked me how I was and I said I was a bit woozy. She said they were going to put me in the corner of the ward next to the nursery so that I would have room to move about in my wheelchair when I eventually got up. So I was moved and the curtains were pulled round me. At the time I didn't mind as all I did was sleep. After the third day I felt better so I asked the nurses if I could have the curtains drawn back but I was told it would be better to leave the curtains as they were for the time being. I felt very upset and isolated as I saw the mums pushing their babies back and forward to the nursery and talking to each other.

When my son, who we named Peter, cried I had to rely on the nurses to get him or change him as the crib moved around on wheels and it was dangerous for me to try on my own. At feeding times the nurse used to come and plonk Peter in my arms, attach him to the breast, leave me for 15 minutes and then rush back and change sides. I was okay with the baby on my left side but I needed help with the right. The nurses were, as usual, short staffed. My right arm made involuntary movements so my son was going up and down while I was feeding him. He looked highly uncomfortable and I wasn't at ease doing it. When I asked for help it was always 'In a minute', which turned out to be at least 20. I used to cuddle my son and tell him how we'd be going home soon and things would be okay. In my mind's eye I had sorted how I was going to cope with breastfeeding Peter and doing things for him once we were home. Here he was waking up every two hours wanting a feed but we would have to wait another 2 hours, which wasn't fair. If a nurse came by I would get her to lift Peter out for me so that I could cuddle him. I would give him a little crafty feed on the left side but I was panicking in case a nurse came and caught me.

On the fourth day I asked if I could have a shower and go to the loo. A nurse came with me as it was my first time out of bed since Peter was born. My wheelchair couldn't fit into the bathroom because the doors were too narrow, so I suggested that I use the shower and loo down at the ante-natal ward, but I was told firmly, 'No'. They said I would have to keep having bedpans and bedbaths, which made me feel twice as powerless as I was feeling already.

Anyway, one morning Peter was screaming his head off as his feed was due at 10 a.m. and by 10.20 nobody had come. I felt Peter and he was drenched. I'd had enough of waiting, so I knelt on my bed and drew the crib as close as I could, then put my left hand under Peter and started to lift him out. Suddenly the crib moved away and I was left outstretched over the bed still holding Peter in the crib. I was like that for ten minutes before a nurse appeared and then I was told off as if I were a child. I found quite a number of nurses on the ward treated me as if I was simple, which aggravated me, but I had to bite my tongue for my baby's sake as I needed their help and support.

On the seventh day my consultant returned from his Easter break and said, 'I told you to wait for me.' I said that I wished I had and began to tell him how I felt about everything. He was so cross that the curtains had been pulled round me all the time. The nurses dug out a crib without wheels that I could use which was much better and the curtains were drawn back so at last I could see and talk to the other mums. I was beginning to feel human again, but I was still eager to go home as the longer I stayed, the more the courage that I had built up for coping with Peter at home slowly ebbed away.

That night some new night staff came. They were very nice and the nurse told me that I should breastfeed my son whatever way I felt comfortable. She showed me how I could feed Peter properly on the right side so that we were both relaxed. We tucked Peter in bed tightly with me while I lay on the right side letting my breast flop just above his face so he could easily latch onto it himself when he wanted to and let it go if he needed a rest. This is how I was planning to feed Peter when I got him home. But the day staff didn't want me to feed Peter with him lying beside me so I had to continue as before until I could go home, which couldn't come quick enough for me.

On the tenth day I had my stitches out. I said to the nurse, 'That means I can go home now,' as I had seen mums who had their stitches out going home within an hour. Fifteen minutes later the sister came to me and said, 'We've just been talking about you. We realise you're eager to go home but we think it would be wiser if you stayed with us until your son is about ten weeks old. We'll bring his own cot from home and some other things so you can show us if you can manage as we have been doing everything for you so far.' I told her that everything was out of my reach here, plus I wasn't allowed to feed Peter the way I wanted to, plus I found things uncomfortable and I would like to go home that evening when my husband and friend came.

She said they weren't ready to discharge me, so I said, 'I'm sorry but if I don't go tonight I will lose all my courage to cope with Peter at home.' So I had to sign my own discharge forms.

The consultant came to say cheerio, which was nice of him, and I felt that he understood my decision. He gave me an appointment to see him with Peter six weeks later. Then at 7 p.m. my friend and husband took me home.

Tehilah: Our Answered Prayer

Chava Willig Levy

My name – Chava – means 'mother of all living' in Hebrew. As a little girl, I remember learning from my parents, both deeply religious Jews, that names are very meaningful. Quoting the Jewish sages of long ago, they told me that parents are granted a moment of prophecy when they choose their new-born's name.

I took their words to heart. Not surprisingly, children have always made me weak in the knees. The fact that a 1955 bout of polio made me *very* weak in the knees never deterred me from my dreams of motherhood.

At 15, I remember asking my doctors, 'Will I be able to have children?' They explained that polio had no effect on the reproductive system; getting pregnant, they implied, would be no problem. 'But, young lady,' and here their voices grew ominous, 'your pelvis is deformed and your breathing is restricted. These polio-related factors could jeopardize a pregnancy. And let's not forget your arms; they're too weak to care for or carry a baby.' One doctor found my question amusing. 'Aren't you putting the cart before the horse? First, see if you can find a husband; then worry about having a baby!' His voice insinuated that my chances for marriage were slim. By the time I was 30, I was beginning to think he was right. My social life in the Big Apple was active, but my dating life was nearly non-existent. Then, in 1982, a miracle happened: I met a wonderful man named Michael Levy. We began dating that December, during the Chanukah season.

What a glorious Chanukah that was! We were head over heels in love, learning how many things we had in common: similar religious values, a passion for words and music and, since Michael is blind, hands-on experience with disability. Married in August, we prayed that God would grant us our deepest wish: to bring a child into His world.

Cushioned by a euphoria common to newly-weds, we were amused when people – even doctors! – asked us if we had consummated our marriage. Amusement turned into annoyance when some people said that, given our disabilities, we'd be irresponsible if we went ahead and had a baby. And in November 1984, when doctors informed us that – due to infertility problems unrelated to our disabilities – our chances of having a child were nearly nil, we were engulfed by anguish.

That Chanukah, still stunned by the doctor's verdict, we hardly felt like celebrating. Each night, as I lit the menorah and recited the blessing, 'Blessed are You, our Lord, who created miracles for our ancestors, in days gone by and in our own time,' I could barely hold back the tears. Would the miracle we prayed for ever come our way?

Three months later, I was pregnant.

Our jubilation knew no bounds. The doctors groped for scientific explanations, but as far as we were concerned, this was the miracle we had been hoping for. We kept our thrilling secret to ourselves for the first three months and then, bursting with joy, we broke our news to the world at large.

Perhaps we shouldn't have, because at the end of my third month, we lost our baby. My obstetrician explained that I had a blighted ovum, a fertilized egg that never developed. The hormones it produced made me look and feel pregnant, but in fact there was no baby growing inside me after all.

This emotional rollercoaster ride sent us reeling. We struggled with painful questions – Why did this happen to us? What did we do to deserve this agony? If we were not meant to have children, why would God 'tease' us with such short-lived joy? We tried to keep our faith and trust that God's love, although hidden, was still with us.

Then on 26 February 1986, nine months and four days after our miscarriage, Michael and I learned that I was pregnant once again. Two days earlier, my younger brother and his wife had had their fifth child who, by higher mathematics, was conceived just when our first conception faltered and failed. After months of mourning and attempting to make sense of our loss, I felt that all was right in the world once more. There was a God in the universe after all, and He had decided that in our family tree, another life had to precede our little one's arrival.

My optimism swelled the next day when a man and his three-year-old son passed me in the street and noticed me struggling to get myself and my motorized wheelchair into a taxi. Without a moment's hesitation, the man brought his son over to me, placed the boy's hand in mine, and told him, 'Now, hold on to this lady. I'll be right back.' While he proceeded to put my wheelchair into the cab, I marveled at the feel of this child's hand in mine, the look of his lovely face, the sound of his barely audible voice when I asked his name. It was a sign, I remember thinking as I looked at my deformed hand holding his and noticed how he didn't pull away. This time the little one wouldn't leave me.

A few hours later, I headed to my gynecologist's office for the official blood test (a home pregnancy test had given us the glorious news). On the way, I passed a little gift shop. Attracted by a glass candlestick in the window, I decided to pop inside and treat myself to it. I made my purchase and was about to leave when I noticed, on the back wall, a display of children's puppet-washcloths shaped like various animals. The variety was impressive – pigs, roosters, bulls, mice, frogs – but the moment I spotted the pink and white lamb, I knew what my selection would be. On our second date, my husband had shared with me a children's poem about a lamb, and it had figured prominently in our courtship – as it still does in our marriage. So I bought all the lambs in the store: one for my new niece, the others for all the babies our friends were expecting, and one for our little one.

The next day, I started staining. My euphoria turned to dread. Silently, I begged our little one, 'Please don't leave us. It's been only two days, but we love you so much already.' It took several weeks to discover that I had an ectopic pregnancy. The embryo was growing in my fallopian tube; if left unchecked it could have killed me. Ectopic pregnancies are usually terminated surgically. But because anesthesia restricts my breathing, I spent a week undergoing a new drug treatment that dissolved my life-threatening embryo. The doctor told me that once a woman has had an ectopic pregnancy, she is less likely to have a baby.

It took several months to recover from our loss, but Michael and I were soon back on the infertility circuit. Month after month came a series of blood tests, sonograms, hormone medications and doctor's appointments. Month after month, my supply of lamb washcloths dwindled as relatives and friends had babies; when only one remained, I tucked it away next to Michael's love letters, suspecting it would stay there for ever.

By the time Chanukah of 1988 rolled around, I was overwhelmed by frustration and fatigue. I remember turning to Michael, the most supportive husband in the world, and saying, 'I've never been one to cut my losses, but I can't keep banging my head against the wall. Do you think we could look into adoption?' That January, after consulting with an adoption attorney, we placed ads across the country and waited by our new phone line, hoping to hear from a pregnant woman in need of our help. The calls were few and fruitless.

In mid-February, in need of a break, we decided to spend a few days in Florida, visiting Michael's parents. While there, I got my period. The usual disappointment turned to dread when I noticed that the flow was barely a trickle, similar to my ectopic symptoms. As we flew home, I said to Michael, 'I don't care if New York is battling a blizzard. First thing tomorrow, I'm going for a blood test. I can't have this anxiety hanging over my head.'

The next morning, I made my way across town to the lab where I'd gone so often. All I wanted to hear was that I did not have an ectopic pregnancy; that this strange period was perhaps a reaction to air travel. That afternoon, just as I was about to light the Sabbath candles, the phone rang. 'Congratulations, Mrs Levy. You're pregnant!' a cheery voice announced.

'That's impossible! I've got my period,' I whispered. 'And besides, we stopped all fertility procedures and medications two months ago!'

'There's no doubt about it: you're definitely pregnant. Some women do get a period during their first month; that's why they often miscalculate their due date. As for your due date, it looks like it will be at the end of October.'

Following that extraordinary phone call, Michael and I were too stunned to speak. We sat together and, with tears in our eyes, prayed that this time the Almighty would help us bring a child into His world.

He did. The pregnancy had its rough moments – a month of bedrest, a bad fall in my eighth month, breathing and sleeping problems, a cesarean section – but God did not abandon us. (Neither did our many friends and relatives whose prayers, good deeds and optimism helped us through many months of anxiety and anticipation.) On 17 October 1989 our beautiful daughter was born. We named her Tehilah Sarah. Tehilah means many things: praise, a song, a poem to God. And the Bible paints a poignant picture of Sarah (a name shared by my two grandmothers), the matriarch heartbroken by childlessness who nevertheless lived to build a dynasty.

Today, as I watch our little one blossom, I remember my doctor's dire prediction: 'And let's not forget your arms; they're too weak to care for or carry a baby.' He was half-right: I can't carry Tehilah, but I can care for her. When Michael is home, we can manage pretty well, each of us compensating for the other's disability. Diapering Tehilah, for example, can be quite an adventure. Michael lifts her onto the changing table, unfastens her diaper and holds her legs while I wipe her and apply Desitin. If Tehilah is really dirty, we reach for her lamb washcloth, hidden away for so many years. As she squeals with glee and tries to grab it, joy overwhelms us.

Because Michael's job takes him away, we have hired a full-time babysitter/housekeeper. She and I work as partners. At mealtimes, she lifts Tehilah into her high chair and brings me her food so that I can feed her. When it's time for Tehilah's bottle, I lie down and Tehilah is placed on my stomach. Our babysitter puts a small pillow under my wrist so that the bottle stays at the proper angle. These tasks are tiring, but I wouldn't relinquish them for the world.

When Tehilah was seven months old, I actually discovered that I can carry my little girl with the help of a baby carrier called Sara's Ride. We originally purchased it with Michael in mind, figuring he could carry Tehilah on his hip and still get around unencumbered with his cane. Well, as it turns out, Michael rarely uses the device. I, on the other hand, have begun to carry Tehilah around on my own! I sit in my motorized scooter and, once Tehilah is secured on my lap, we roam the streets of New York unaccompanied! After an hour or so, fatigue sets in – but how thrilling it is to feel so truly united with my daughter, with no one hovering nearby to intervene. At day's end, we often head for Broadway and wait for Michael to emerge from the subway station. When Tehilah spots her Abba (Hebrew for Daddy) approaching, she gurgles excitedly. Michael stops in his tracks and, when I verbally second her emotion, he beams with delight. Passersby, notorious in New York for keeping their distance, smile at us as we head for home.

People often ask us if Tehilah knows yet that her parents have disabilities. The answer is yes – and no. When she was only seven months old, I discovered that Tehilah's 'pick-me-up' plea, indicated by arms stretched eagerly upward, is never directed to me. And one evening, when she was eight months old, Tehilah started whimpering while the three of us were watching a television game show. We had no idea what was wrong. Suddenly, our unhappy little girl craned her neck until she located me. She gave me a pleading look, turned back toward Michael and then my way once more. 'Michael,' I said, 'could it be that you're blocking her view of the TV screen?' Michael moved slightly to his left and Tehilah was content once more. More interesting than our daughter's fascination with game shows is her awareness that visual obstacles are easier to resolve with her mother's intervention.

So yes, Tehilah has learned that her parents have disabilities. But she has not learned that, in the eyes of most people, her parents are 'different' or even 'unfortunate'. Seeing a wheelchair, a braille book, unfocused eyes or an asymmetrical body is commonplace for our little girl. And, speaking candidly, Michael and I think that makes Tehilah a very fortunate person. As she gets older, she will discover society's misconceptions about disability. But, happily, children and adults who lack Tehilah's enlightened upbringing will encounter a refreshingly bemused response from our little girl. We pray that Tehilah will teach them all that disability need not be an obstacle to successful parenthood.

As Michael and I anticipate Tehilah's second Chanukah, we remember the Chanukahs that have come before. This year as I light the menorah for my husband and daughter, I know my eyes will well up once again – this time with tears of thanksgiving.

Reclamation

Micheline Mason

It seems so natural now that pregnant women are screened for 'abnormal' foetuses, and that doctors should have the power they do, that it is hard to imagine that this is a modern phenomenon, only existing in highly developed, technologically obsessed, profit-orientated societies. In Britain, it was only after 1913 that doctors were designated by the State the role of separating out the 'deserving' from the 'undeserving' poor through the implementation of the Mental Defectives Act. This Act created several categories of 'defective' people, ranging from 'cretins' to 'moral defectives'. Doctors were asked to examine suspects, write reports, and recommend 'placement'. This placement could include long-term incarceration in a hospital or home.

Children were not spared this vetting. Parents were seen as a big problem because they often persisted in loving their children and believing they were human, even when they had impairments. This led many parents to be reluctant to 'let them go', and hospital staff were trained to try and stop the bonding before it had begun. They moved new-born babies to separate nurseries, did not encourage the parents to see or hold the baby, and urged them to leave them behind to be put into care. 'Go home and have another baby' was the wisdom of the time.

The breaking of the relationships between disabled and non-disabled people has been our national policy for nearly one hundred years.

It has been a very difficult process reclaiming myself from this legacy.

The medical profession created words to describe my body. The words they used, without a moment's reflection as to how these words would destroy my sense of self, were 'deformed', 'abnormal', 'misshapen', 'severely handi-capped', 'fragile', 'invalid'. They used them whilst standing looking at negative images of various parts of my skeleton, tutting and sighing. No one said 'pretty', 'attractive', 'unique', 'sensitive', or 'warm', although I was also all of those things. Instead they brought droves of medical students to study my sad bits, my 'thin sclerotic linings'; to have fun guessing what it was that was 'wrong' with me.

Once a medical photographer came to my bedside. I had combed my hair and put on my sweetest seven-year-old smile in preparation. When he put the screens around my bed and asked me to take off my nightie, I was dismayed. When he took close-ups of my arms, my legs, my back, without once including my head, I was shocked beyond measure. He said they were going into a book for medical students. If he had asked me, I would have said no. I could not bear the thought of being visually dismembered, nameless and headless in a book for all to see. They would learn nothing about me from such pictures.

It was a long journey from being 'cut up' by a medical photographer, to being confident enough to consider becoming a parent. Even now I am not sure that I would have made the decision from scratch. In the event, the only decision I had to make was whether or not to continue with an accidental pregnancy. I had deliberately avoided asking for 'advice' from any medical person as to the wisdom or not of my becoming a mother. I knew from past experience that all I would hear would be their fears and prejudices. I had found out though, that any child I had would have a 50 per cent chance of inheriting my condition and had spent several years working out what I thought about this. By the time I was faced with the real possibility, I knew that a disabled child's life would be of at least the same value as my own, and they therefore had every right to live it. I also thought I could protect a disabled child better than most from the oppression they would face. I was much more concerned about myself and my circumstances, including the fact that I would become a lone parent, and of this I was truly afraid.

Yet, I had often been afraid in my life, and had never let it get the better of me. I chose life, and 'life' looked after me as it had always done. From the moment of decision, a protective mechanism seemed to enfold me. I surrounded myself with people who could and would be positive about this new life within me. I avoided the doubters and sceptics as much as possible, and if I could not avoid them, because I was related to them, or they were my GP, I took a 'bodyguard' with me. I smiled at them all. I did not ask for reassurance from them, I just needed their skills, their cooperation. I told them that *they* must prepare for the possibility of a disabled baby, not to bother me with any form of 'screening', and not to share their worries with me. I am sure that by presenting them all with a fait accompli, I side-stepped the negative reaction which has been the experience of many of my disabled friends.

I am only 3ft tall and I am not straight or symmetrical anywhere. In this light, it is amazing that 'What! You're too small to have a baby!', blurted out by my shocked GP, was the only really negative remark made in the whole nine months. Looking back, most of my memories are of people being excited in some quite profound way. It was as though I was defying their own demons, their own fears and self-imposed limits. Perhaps it was that 'oppressed' person within all of us realising that we do not have to give in.

For my part, a certain amount of bravado was involved. I was anxious about the birth, and about the rest of our life together, especially when a late scan did confirm the fact that the baby had inherited my condition of brittle bones. My tears and panics were kept for a very small group of friends who could listen to me without 'joining in'. In fact, I think I became a bit ruthless as the pregnancy progressed, pruning the list of acceptable visitors to a rather narrow selection of about two, but I felt it was a necessary form of self-defence, and was only for a short period of time.

The last six weeks of my pregnancy, and Lucy's birth, were, by necessity, very closely monitored. I was asked to come into hospital for that time and it was difficult then to remember that I was not ill. I was surrounded by women who were worried about their own pregnancies, and each one had a story to tell. I, with my attempt to remain calm and confident, became a sitting target. I began knitting classes by my bedside in order to try and distract them, but it was not wholly successful as a tactic.

I hated the daily foetal heart monitoring, and the blood tests, which were an unavoidable part of the ward routine. The consultant, however, was always encouraging and reassuring and in this I know I was unusually fortunate. 'Nature is wonderful!' he said to his students as he showed them how the baby had taken up a sideways position instead of the expected up-and-down one. This prevented most of the things about which he had been concerned – that my breathing would become restricted, or the baby would feel squashed and decide to be born early. It did cause another problem of how they were going to get her out, but he seemed to treat this as an interesting challenge rather than an enormous difficulty. The positive nature of his approach only really came home to me when he shared with me his dilemma of which angle to make the incision – vertically or horizontally. The easiest for him would be a vertical cut, but this worried him because it could mean I could only have two children, whereas a horizontal approach would enable me to have four!

Many women talk of a caesarean as unnatural, feeling somehow cheated out of a real birth, but I did not feel like that. For the first time in my life I felt as though the medical profession were using their highly developed skills to help me achieve something I truly wanted. In fact without their skills neither of us could have survived. I cannot help but feel grateful that I live in a 'rich' country where such help is available.

My long stay did mean that half the hospital knew about us and wanted to see this baby as soon as she was born. I remember the sound of the mobile incubator wheeling along from the Special Care Baby Unit, with a beautiful bright-eyed baby only two hours old, and an entourage of nurses, friends and domestic staff, laughing, admiring, planning little gifts and asking if they could bring their relatives to see her. I contrasted this with the sense of tragedy and sorrow that had surrounded my own early days, and wondered what had made the difference. It certainly could not be explained simply by the fact that it was 32 years later. I know that disabled infants are still greeted with shock and misery most of the time. Was it because I was able to welcome her completely, including her impairment, that allowed everyone else to follow suit? For me, it was the unknown factors of our life ahead which were frightening, not the known hand of cards with which I had been dealt. After all, I knew all about brittle bones already whereas most people know very little. For most, the reality of any impairment which is not one you have yourself, is a leap in the dark. In the absence of close relationships with disabled people, which is still true for the majority of the population, the dreadful legacy of the past with its eugenic undertones thoroughly distorts our view of disability, leading us endlessly back into the circle of fear, exclusion, ignorance, fear.

Lucy is now 14 years old, a very strong young woman in her own right. We have ridden the wave of 'integrated education', and she has never known the physical separation from her mother, or her community, with which I had to contend. But her world is still unsafe, her place in it still conditional on the judgement of medical professionals. Many of her disabled peers are not by her side in mainstream society, but are still in segregated institutions of all kinds, put there by the non-disabled world. We both still need our circle of friends to remind us that our battle is not just for us, but for all of us; for the whole of humanity.

Are You Sure You Can Cope?

Michele Wates

Disabled parents, spearheaded by disabled mothers, are choosing to become visible, not because it is finally safe to do so or because prejudice and discrimination are things of the past, but rather because we recognise the power of being visible as a group. Creating an effective information and peer support network has had a direct effect on the amount and the quality of support available to new and prospective disabled parents.

For me this has been a personal as much as a political journey. When I was first diagnosed, at the age of 27, as having multiple sclerosis, it never occurred to me to find out whether any specific support was available to disabled parents, either from statutory sources or through the voluntary sector. If offers of support had been made, I might not have taken them up in any case. Up to this point I had never been part of any organisation or support group that had disability as its focus and this was, in part, because I felt uncomfortable about thinking of myself as a disabled person.

However, the effects of the illness were becoming increasingly apparent as my walking became laboured and erratic, and the likelihood was that my condition would continue to worsen. I had to consider the difficulties that might arise if I were to have a second child. How would I feel about my increasing need for support? How would I respond to any suggestion that I was being less than responsible in having another child?

I had the feeling, without being able to say exactly why, that disabled mothers were assumed to be problem mothers or 'at risk' in some way. Yet my own limited experience suggested to me that there are certain

94

distinctive *strengths* in the parenting styles of disabled people. For example, I had noticed that I found it necessary, and therefore natural, to involve other people in the day to day tasks of looking after and entertaining my small son. This made parenting a more companionable experience for me and enriched his life too. A growing interest in meeting with women who were facing issues and challenges similar to my own coincided with an interest in posing a question that seemed not to have been asked before – 'In what ways do disabled people make particularly *good* parents?'

It soon became clear that it was going to be harder than I had thought to make contact with other parents. The wind was further knocked out of my sails during my first interview with another disabled mother, when I explained that I was hoping to write the findings up in a book and she responded dubiously, 'I hope it isn't going to be another of those books about heroines.' On reflection, I took her point. The media loves to present the lives of disabled people in terms of how *exceptional* they are, their bravery and determination in the face of adversity and tragedy, and so on. At the same time there is a contrasting, but equally artificial, tendency to blame disabled people for being so *irresponsible* as to have children.

The apparent contradiction between praising and blaming is not as great as it seems since the effect of both is to distance disabled parents from our non-disabled peers. I was finding that disabled parents do not want to be singled out, whether for praise, blame or sympathy. Tensions emerged between standing out and blending in, between highlighting and side-lining, between celebration and blame, letting needs be known and keeping them hidden.

So what is the reality? Are our families characterised by their normality or by their exceptionality? Are we concerned with merging into the mainstream or are we signalling a way forward; creating styles of parenting that are less isolated, more comfortable with difference and that richly foster the skills of interdependence?

I was struck by the number of times disabled parents spoke of the desire to 'live as normal a life as possible', 'to do the things normal families do'. What happens to that hankering after 'normality' once we have come together as disabled parents, countered the sense of isolation and exposure that made it seem unsafe to be different, and taken on the task of self-representation? Does it fall away? Well, yes and no. Yes, in the sense that it leaves us free to get on with the pains and pleasures of living with our children. Yes, in the sense that we are relieved of the need to justify our parenting on non-disabled terms, and yes, in the sense that we can begin to take full pride in our own distinctive styles of parenting. But, no, the aspiration to be treated as 'normal' does not fall away, so long as disabled people have restricted access to everyday facilities and services designed for parents and families.

The coming together of disabled mothers, and to a lesser extent disabled fathers, is one strand in what has been identified as a national and international movement of self-realisation and empowerment amongst disabled people. The transition from passively experiencing disadvantage to actively contributing to its elimination, is a powerful transformation in the lives of individuals and in society as a whole.

We no longer accept seeing ourselves as a sub-group of parents who have somehow slipped through the net and had better watch our step. We had a right to become parents in the first place and we have the right to be adequately and appropriately resourced for the task. We are ordinary parents and at the same time we have particular insights and qualities that we have developed in our parenting.

One thing that is clear is that it does not make sense to go after a supposed normality that involves us in continuous and uncomplaining struggle. It doesn't make sense for us, and it doesn't make sense for the rest of society either. Disabled people are amongst those most severely affected by the under-resourcing, poor moral support, unwelcoming attitudes and inappropriate physical design which to a greater or lesser extent affect the lives of all parents of young children. Drawing attention to the barriers and prejudices faced by *disabled* parents would benefit everyone.

The time has come to turn around the question that so many of us were asked when we first told families, friends and health professionals that we were going to become mothers: are you sure *you* can cope?

Part III
Along the Way

The Seeds of Trust

Denise Sherer Jacobson

Just a few more blocks. My back ached badly now and David, sitting on my lap at this hour of the late afternoon, felt as heavy as the 40 pounds he weighed. We passed the entrance to Grand Auto and neared the rounded corner of Broadway and 51st. It was not one of my favorite crossings. Traffic came from all directions. Lights and arrows changed at the blink of an eye. Cars breezed through the narrow turn-off between the curb cut and the triangular island that I had to reach before crossing the wide thoroughfares of either Broadway or 51st.

David had stopped singing. He was bent over the right armrest of my chair watching the wheels go round. The motion had fascinated him ever since he was a baby. He seemed to be leaning a little further over than usual, and I thought about saying something, but the right turn lane was clearing. I saw our opportunity to make the first leg of that precarious crossing.

I started, only to be stopped – just as we made it to the edge of the island – by the piercing shrieks of my son. He sprang upright. I was ready to scold him until I saw him holding up the middle finger of his right hand. It was drenched in crimson blood.

Instinctively my palm pressed forward on the joystick so we would be clear of traffic. My wheelchair squealed laboriously up the curb cut and then rested. I ignored the ominous squeal and examined David's finger to see if it was still all there, knowing that if it wasn't, I'd have to start looking for a little piece of finger, too. The wound was pretty deep but the finger tip was still there, joint and all.

'It's gonna be okay, David,' I tried to soothe above his

hysterical cry. His tongue quivered as tears rolled down his soft round cheeks. 'You'll be fine. You'll be fine.'

On the corner we had just came from, I spotted a young girl wearing the plaid uniform of St Theresa's high school. She was on her way over.

'We can go back in there and wash it off,' she suggested, nodding in the direction of Grand Auto.

My wheelchair inched back across the street, barely making it up the curb, but the girl didn't realize I was having trouble. 'Here,' she said taking David by the hand, 'I'll take him in.'

Reluctantly I had to agree to let him go with this stranger. There seemed to be very little forward power on the right side of my wheelchair. I had to back up the slight incline of the doorway. Once I got on the flat vinyl surface I was able to turn and approach one of two bored-looking women at the check-out counter.

'Where's the little boy?' I asked.

'Huh?'

I repeated, 'Where's the little boy?'

'She wants to know where the little boy is,' her co-worker translated.

'Oh . . . They took him to the bathroom,' she answered.

'Where is it?' I demanded.

She turned back to me in a manner revealing no awareness at all of my irritation. 'Oh, follow me.'

She disappeared between the aisle of car gizmos and white-walled tires. I creaked after her, having the first chance to glimpse down over the right side of the wheelchair. I was relieved when I saw what was wrong. The quarter-inch rubber drive belt had come off its track, which ran from the rear wheel around the pulley attached to the right motor in front. David must have dislodged it as he pulled his finger free. It would be a cinch to fix, especially here at Grand Auto!

'I don't think she could get back into the bathroom,' I heard somebody say as I neared a free-standing counter a few feet from the side door. 'He'll be right out, anyway.'

So, the girl didn't take off with him! I breathed with relief, already thinking about whether I should take David home, call the doctor, and find someone to drive us there; or whether I could whiz us straight down to his office a little less than two miles away, in just about the same amount of time. First, however, I needed to have my drive belt realigned or we wouldn't be going anywhere.

I opened my mouth to speak to the man behind the counter but he averted his eyes and started to serve a customer who had just approached him.

Gritting my teeth, I swallowed and waited for him to finish. When he did, he started to turn away.

'Sir. Sir. *SIR*,' I persisted louder and louder until, when others started looking, he could no longer ignore me. 'I need some help with my wheelchair.'

I pointed to the drive belt. He barely bent down to give it a look before calling over a man in overalls. Then he walked back behind the counter, leaving me to explain what needed to be done. In the midst of my efforts, David came out of the bathroom. His howling grew louder as he approached. I heard voices talking to him, trying to console him.

'Your finger will be all right, son.'

'They'll be here soon. They'll make it better.'

'They' sounded ominous, but at the moment I was too involved even to ask who *they* were. David, his injured finger wrapped in a brown paper towel, stepped up on my footrests, straddled my left leg and settled into my lap. Tears streamed down his cheeks. I wanted to comfort him, yet his cries were interrupting my attempt at directing the two auto mechanics now working on getting the quarter-inch drive belt back in place. It was so simple. I had watched it being done so many times before at the wheelchair repair shop. I had told friends how to do it when I had belt trouble at home. But now with David sobbing on my lap, a small crowd fussing over him, and baffled repairmen flanking my wheel-chair, I couldn't remember whether the belt should be slipped around the back wheel or front pulley first.

I desperately needed my wheelchair working again, so that we could get out of there before 'they' came. As it turned out, both happened at the same time.

The same woman clerk led the two paramedics to us. The blond-haired one squatted down in front of David. The bearded dark-haired one with glasses stood beside him, hands on hips.

'She his mother?' the bearded one asked.

Who the hell else would I be?

Someone answered yes.

'What's his name?' the one who squatted asked.

'David,' I replied.

'David, can I see your finger?'

'No!' he howled through tears.

'David, honey, you need to show him your finger,' I coaxed in a deliberately calm voice.

My son looked at me with swollen, watery eyes, then put out his wrapped finger. The paramedic unwrapped it with slow gentleness.

'Looks pretty bad,' he said.

After examining the finger, he raised his eyes to his partner. 'Here, take a look.'

'Geez, looks like the tip of it is gone.'

Could I have been wrong? I peeked over David's shoulder; the finger still looked the same to me.

David started crying again.

'He'll probably need stitches,' the bearded one said as he stood up. 'Let's get him to the hospital.'

'No,' I protested immediately. 'I'll take him to his doctor.'

'We can't let you do that.'

'Why not?'

'He needs immediate attention.'

'I'll get there in ten minutes,' I lied.

The two paramedics gave each other wary glances, indicating they had no intention of letting us go anywhere. The blond one spoke. 'We need to fill out some paperwork. Why don't I go get it and David could come out to get his finger bandaged?'

Instinctively my arm tightened around David's waist, although he made no move to get up. In fact, he scooted back further into my lap.

'We'll both go with you.' I started to move.

'No, you stay here.' His placating tone sounded very suspicious.

I didn't listen. They wanted to take my child away from me. My years of experience as a helpless child with intimidated parents in the medical world had clued me in. I wasn't naive. We were *all* going outside!

When their tactic of trying to separate us didn't work, the paramedics pressured me again as they towered over me in the corner parking lot. 'We need to take him to the hospital.'

'And what about me?' I questioned defiantly. 'How will I get there?'

A look at me and then at each other told me they hadn't thought about that. The bearded one suggested, 'We could call a paddy wagon for her.'

'For her,' I assumed meant they would still take David in the ambulance. I couldn't let that happen. 'No!'

If David had been profusely bleeding, his arm dangling with an obvious break, or had he been unconscious, I would have immediately sent him off with them. But my son had squarely planted himself on my lap; even his tears had stopped. I had no idea what he made of all this chaos, but I knew that if I let them take him now, David's trust in me would begin to waver. I remembered so long ago, myself as a three-year-old, crying so hysterically while my mother – coaxed by hospital staff – walked down the dim corridor and disappeared. She came back for visiting day two days later and to take me home on weekends during my three week hospital stay, but the seed of mistrust had already been sown – a seed that has haunted me all my life.

A small crowd had followed us outside. The two paramedics had turned slightly from me to have a tête-àtête. They spoke in low voices, but as a practiced eavesdropper my whole life long, I adeptly filtered out the noisy traffic and the murmurs of onlookers to catch their words. 'We'll have to call the police,' the blond said to the nodding beard.

Like a bad dream, this was getting more and more out of control. I clearly had no credibility. I had to call someone who could get them to see the reality of the situation. But who? Neil in this case was not a likely choice. If I was being dismissed as a raving cripple, the chances were that he would be too.

'Look, call my doctor,' I desperately implored, getting them to at least look at me again. 'Please, don't call the police...Call my doctor.'

The repairman, who had fixed my drive belt, knelt on the other side of me. He spoke in a tone as if he were admonishing a child. 'You don't understand, he needs to go to the hospital.'

'No, *you* don't understand!' I answered back in a voice from deep inside me, articulated with strength and clarity I never knew I had. 'He's not going anywhere without me!'

Surprisingly, the man, as well as the rest of the small group that had gathered around us, seemed to retreat somewhat from the force of my words.

I strained my head, searching the crowd for sympathetic eyes. The paramedics stood over me. They still weren't listening. They made some effort to coax David out of my lap. He remained amazingly steadfast. *Did he comprehend some of what was going on or did his instinct warn him?*

I made eye contact with the girl in the uniform again, and, for the second time, she came to my rescue. Borrowing a small pad from the repairman and a pen from the bearded paramedic who was busily informing his partner that he had just radioed the police, she wrote down the number I gave her and our last name. Then she disappeared. I prayed she would get the call through before the police arrived.

A few minutes later, the girl reappeared into the small muddled crowd and announced, 'The doctor would like to speak to one of the paramedics!'

Suddenly, a hush settled over the crowd, as if everyone had been slapped into sense. The bearded paramedic went to take the phone call. The crowd dispersed, leaving the other paramedic to squat down to my eye level and finally speak to me as a human being.

'We'll do whatever the doctor says,' he now assured me.

'That's fine,' I said. 'We'll go wherever he thinks we should go. Right David?'

David turned to me first and then nodded to the paramedic. He had calmed down soon after everyone left. Even his dry sobs began to ebb.

I was almost certain that we would end up being sent to the hospital if the other paramedic had described David's finger as he saw it. I intended to pursue an agreeable course of action. 'How will we get there?'

His answer surprised me. He had actually thought it out. 'We could lift David and you onto the stretcher and put your chair up front next to the driver's seat.'

What a difference a minute could make!

The bearded paramedic returned with the news I had expected. 'The doctor said you probably should go to the hospital because David will most likely need stitches and X-rays.'

'Okay,' I nodded, giving David a reassuring squeeze. 'We're ready whenever you are.'

First the bearded paramedic had to explain to the policeman who just arrived in his squad car that his services weren't required.

'Wow, David, this is your first ride in an ambulance,' I said as they were loading us on.

'And hopefully your last!' the blond paramedic added, echoing my unspoken sentiment.

Our eyes caught one another's. We smiled to acknowledge our similar thinking. I never would have suspected that, propped up on a stretcher in an ambulance with my four-and-a-half-year-old son resting contentedly on top of me, I could feel so very much in control.

Role Reversal

Catherine Bradbury

I arrive in a taxi, silently sobbing.
My daughter welcomes me.
'Oh Mum...'
And these two words
Wrap me round
With her love and concern.

I see her groping
For a way to tear off
The all-embracing hopelessness:
Haul me from this deep, dark place;
Bring me to a cool, clear light -
While I stand there, rocking from foot to foot,
Adrift in an altered dimension.

I dog her footsteps
Through the time-laden day
And she needs respite.
Gently, as with a small child,
She tells me to go and have a bath.

'Shall we go out with my friends tonight?
I've warned them you're a bit odd.'

Sitting in the pub

Half-heard hub-bub
Of other people's lives,
A never-ending
Light opera

Dark opera

Stifling the tears
As the girl in the band
Happily sings
'Won't you please, please help me?'

In My Mind's Eye: III
Early days of parenting

Jo Litwinowicz

Once the initial shock of being home wore off and I was busy looking after my new baby, I forgot my worries. The day after I came home our doctor and midwife came round saying, 'You left your mark by signing yourself out of hospital. Good for you!' My doctor understood why I had done it, as once I had worked things out in my mind, I had to be given the chance to carry them out as soon as I could. We sat down and decided that the midwife would come in twice a day for eight weeks and that the warden would pop in four times a day or when I needed help to change Peter.

My husband had two weeks off work without pay to get to know our son. Money was tight. My mobility allowance helped to pay for a home help three times a week. At that time I didn't even have a washing machine so I was doing all the washing by hand and with the nappies it was hard work!

After about three weeks of being at home I had a visit from a market researcher. She asked if I would help by trying out different kinds of disposable nappies, so I agreed. That way I would be able to see if I could manage them myself and if I couldn't, it wouldn't be money down the drain. I was given 24 nappies each week and every week they brought me a different make. This lasted for seven weeks which was extremely handy. When my husband wasn't around I used the disposables but during the evenings and nights and at weekends we used cloth nappies. It also meant that there were fewer nappies to wash. By the end of the trials I had saved a few disposables which I was able to use till they ran out. I found them easy to use but once the sticky tape was stuck you had a job to undo it and Peter wriggled so much it more or less stuck to everything!

When a baby comes into the family unit the husband sometimes feels pushed out, but in our case I felt I was the intruder. I know I had regretted that my husband wasn't really part of the pregnancy but once I brought Peter home he seemed to take over completely. In a way I was grateful as I was too frightened to pick Peter up and carry him, bath him, dress him or undress him. At first he looked so small and helpless and I felt so heavy handed. I began to feel threatened and jealous of my husband but deep in my heart I knew I couldn't manage without him. Also, a part of me was over the moon that he took to Peter so quickly.

After two weeks at home my husband should have gone back to work but he didn't as I felt more secure when he was at home. The doctor came to see me and he told my husband that I could manage and he should go back to work the next day as we couldn't live on air. He turned to me and said, 'Where's all that fighting spirit you had? It's now that you need it, to show everyone you're not all talk. Don't let me down now that I've stuck my neck out for you.'

Next morning Peter woke up at 6 a.m. so my husband washed, changed and dressed him and put him on the bed while I fed him. I got ready whilst my husband put Peter in his pram and then I prepared my husband's breakfast. He went off to work at 7.45. I kept praying that Peter would sleep till the midwife came. He seemed fast asleep so I washed up and got the dinner on. I started on the washing but Peter woke at 9.30 so I took his nappy off and let him be free from it. If Peter was wet then I could easily wash out the pram sheets. I had bought quite a lot of pram and cot sheets and blankets as I knew there would be accidents and I wanted to be prepared. It was much easier changing the little sheets than a nappy.

Once my husband put Peter in his pram each morning

that's where he remained. I used to breastfeed over the side of the pram so Peter could latch on with ease and I could cuddle him and talk to him at the same time without jerking him. When he finished with one breast I went round the other side of the pram and repeated the same thing.

My parents came to see us. They had said over the phone that I should let Peter live with them as he'd have a better chance in life with them than with me. I was constantly afraid that my parents or the authorities would come to my house one day and take Peter from me. I was scared to tell anyone just in case they did take him away. I got more and more depressed but I didn't dare talk about my fear to anyone, not even the doctor.

I knew that I was doing more for my son than even an able-bodied mum, but I thought I still didn't love him as a mum loves her child. It felt wrong. It was as though I was distancing myself and locking up how I really felt about Peter in case someone took him from me, so that if it happened it wouldn't hurt so much. It was a weird thing to feel when really I loved my son!

About seven weeks after coming home the doctor came and found me upset and the whole story came out. He said, 'Stop thinking that anyone will take Peter away from you.' He said that I'd put everyone to shame by showing them that I was a very good mum, better than many able-bodied mums that he knew.

One afternoon when Peter was about ten weeks old he was crying and crying but I knew he didn't need changing or feeding; even cuddling him didn't seem to calm him down. Nobody was expected and I didn't want to call the warden as Peter was my responsibility and if I went running for help every time something happened, they might not come immediately if there was a real emergency. I felt that I could manage, given time, so I said to Peter, 'Mummy's going to try to get you out of the pram so calm down.' It was as though he understood and he quietened down a bit so I pushed the pram close to the settee, got out of the wheelchair and managed to shuffle myself between the pram and the settee. Talking to Peter all the time I rolled him over on his tummy, got a bit of his jumper between my teeth, slid my good hand underneath him and gently lifted him up above the sides of the pram. Then I fell back, praying like mad that I'd end up on the settee and not on the floor. I made it and turned Peter over to see if he'd survived. My heat was in my mouth and thumping but there seemed to be a smile on his face saying, 'There, you did it mum.'

I felt so chuffed that I had my son on my lap; the feeling of holding him close was great. After that I got him out every day for a cuddle and a sing-song but I didn't do it in front of anyone because people might think I was hurting him, besides which I didn't like people watching how I did things at the best of times.

It's funny how babies know you. When I was handling Peter on my own, however rough I was or if I accidentally scratched him, he never protested, but one day my husband was playing with him and accidentally scratched him and he screamed his lungs out.

If Peter slept at all in the day I was lucky. If he slept four hours at a time it was a small miracle. The doctor said he didn't need much sleep. I said, 'Yes but I do!' I was very tired and run down and I wasn't putting on a lot more weight. The consultant said I could have a sterilisation if I didn't want any more children. I was so depressed I wasn't thinking rationally because deep down inside me I wanted another child. But on the other hand I had to rely on a lot of people to rally round and help when Peter was small. Once is okay but if I had another child they might not be so keen. I was so tired that in the end I went into hospital overnight to be sterilised, but I was back home for Peter's afternoon feed.

My husband came home one night and said that he had been talking to his mate and that his mate's wife was a qualified childminder living about ten minutes' walk from our house. He had arranged for them to come and meet me and Peter that evening. Linda came again the next day and asked me to go down to Toddlers with her and meet all the new mums with their children. I was apprehensive because this was going to be the first time I had socialised since I bought Peter home from hospital. The first ten minutes were the worst, then some 18-month-old children came to give me their toys in exchange for playing with the wheels of my chair. When they got a bit more adventurous they began pushing me about. One mum told her child off but I said, 'Don't worry. I'll make sure nothing happens,' and the mum said, 'If we'd known about you we'd have brought you down sooner, then the kids would be content with playing with your chair and we wouldn't have to tidy up the mess.' That broke the ice and I'm still friends with them even though our kids are now 15, 16 and 17.

A Job for Life

Sue Firth

'I think I can remember you showing me how to turn cartwheels on the beach,' said my younger son Tom, 'When your legs worked, before you were poorly.' Hearts don't break, but sometimes it feels as if they crack a little.

I've been a parent for longer than I've been disabled. My illness started when my younger son was three, and by the time he was six I was bedbound. Despite being very ill and feeling that it couldn't get much worse, I continued to deteriorate for a further 12 months, until I reached rock bottom. I was incontinent, unable to feed myself or sit up at all. Tom is now nine and I have improved to the point where I can sit up and eat unaided. I manage the loo by myself most of the time and occasionally get out of bed for a few minutes. However, I am now facing the fact that my illness (ME) appears to be both severe and chronic.

In common with most people who face this kind of illness I see-saw wildly from hope to despair, through all the stages in between. When I despair and look at my life, all I can see is my inability to do the routine things that most people take for granted, the long hours of feeling too ill to do anything, even listening to the radio, and the unhappiness that this generates. Then I have fantasies about two things, being well or being dead.

The first appears little more than a small glow on the horizon; the second is not an option I personally would take because I believe, to paraphrase a common slogan, that children are for life and not just for Christmas. No matter how ill or disabled I am, no matter how independent my kids become, I am still the mother of two lads and they need me – not to do things for them, those days are long gone – they need me just to be here, to be their mother. And when I have what I refer to as 'a bad do', (roughly every 10 to 14 days), when I spend 24 hours semiconscious, doped up on Stemitil and Morphine, lying in the dark, vomiting into a bucket and crying with pain, they still need me. They creep in and lie on the bed for a few minutes saying very little except, 'Luv you Mum.'

For much of my life all I can give them is my presence, my love and my time – time to listen, time to talk, time to laugh, time to cry, time to just be around each other, sharing our lives and hopefully sorting out problems as they occur. My job as a parent hasn't changed since I became disabled, it's just the way I do the job that's changed. I've always felt that my prime objective is to bring the lads up to be able to cope with life and all it throws at you, and that's still what I'm doing when I give them my presence, my time and, most of all, my love.

We are in the very fortunate position at present of my husband being in a reasonably well paid job and so we spend practically all my disability benefit on employing help in the home. This helps in two ways. Firstly the house is cleaned; the washing, ironing and gardening are done on a regular basis, making everything run more smoothly and creating less stress for everyone. Secondly it frees up my husband in the evenings and at weekends to be the active parent, giving the lads his time, taking them to buy trainers, playing football, taxiing them to their social lives, playing chess and so on.

We don't do all this so that our sons have no responsibilities or because we think they are unable to perform household jobs. We do it so that they don't have too many regular jobs; too much responsibility too soon. All children have a right to a childhood. When Mike has to go abroad on business, the lads really respond to the challenge. The elder, 13-year-old Jim, takes on locking up the house, checking that everything's switched off, as well as feeding me, filling hotwater bottles, and other vital tasks before and after school. We employ teenagers in the school holidays to take Tom out swimming, to the pictures, bowling, to the park and mooching round the shops; all the things I'd normally have done.

We also aim for them all, Mike and the boys, to go away on holiday a couple of times a year for five or six days, leaving me to the tender mercies of the local social service department. This is hard. Waving goodbye is the hardest thing in the world. We all cry. It hurts like hell – especially when social services get their wires crossed and the help doesn't come – but it seems to be worth it. They all get a rest from the relentless round of caring for me and the refreshment that comes from seeing different places and doing different things.

Our aim, as you can probably tell, is to have as normal a life as possible for our family. Both lads bring home lots of friends, some of whom cope better with our situation than others (which can be said of adults as well). Some of their mates come and sit on my bed and talk. Some shuffle embarressedly in the doorway. Others merely grunt from the top of the stairs. I asked Jim one day, now that he's getting into his more sensitive teenage years, if I embarrassed him by being disabled. 'Course not,' he said, 'you're ma mum. You just embarrass me, full stop.'

Attitudes in Zambia

Constance Hambwalula

After completing my schooling at the age of 21 years, I was single and without children for another nine years. However, at the age of 30 I was blessed with a son, which was something I rejoiced at. I never felt ashamed of having a child out of wedlock; to me it was a joyful event. It is our custom that when a woman is made pregnant, the man concerned is asked to pay charges and as a woman I was expecting that there would come a time when someone would ask me who was responsible. But up to now (my son is seven years old), none of the relatives on my side have asked me. I don't even know how much that man would have had to pay my parents if I were able-bodied.

Such a development is very sad because this means that my son is unlikely to get help from my relatives in terms of lobola when he wants to marry. The same applies to his schooling. In short my children will not benefit from the wealth of my family nor that of their grandparents.

Four years after the time I had my first-born, I decided to find one who was willing to take me as a wife. My husband and I now have two more children and though we have been together for five years, my parents have not bothered to have this man pay lobola. I'm pretty sure he is not going to be asked to pay my parents anything. A disabled woman is not thought 'woman enough' that someone should pay for her.

The other abnormal thing I have observed from my relatives' behaviour is that despite me having children and a husband, a family of my own, I am still not considered a grown-up woman. I'm not consulted on any family matters if anything goes wrong. Relatives never come to visit me. They would rather visit other people who are younger than me.

This again has its own side effects. My children will not know the family very well which will in turn make it more easy for them to become destitute; in times of difficulty they may have nowhere to turn.

Though my husband is able-bodied, he supports me very much where problems affecting me as a disabled woman are concerned. I'm very thankful that he is able to understand the problems between the able-bodied and the disabled. Because of this, each time he hears of an injustice he tries every means to comfort me and advises me to ignore the people. All the same, I know that ignoring things is not the best way of correcting them.

All in all, I'm a happy disabled mother of three and I will try my level best to put the world straight where matters affecting disabled people are concerned. I feel that, even with my disability, the sky is the limit as long as I am given the freedom to use my rights.

Change for the Hospital Phone

Heather Beattie

My son is asleep and I sit at his side, holding his small hand. My stomach is knotted and I feel sick and tense. The piercing pain around my heart seems palpable, wounding. Tomorrow I will disrupt his serene, peaceful world by telling him that I have to go into hospital again. I know it will hurt him terribly. Everything within me recoils from having to tell him. It never seems to get easier, only harder – more of a sickening dread inside me each time I go to shatter his world.

I love Connor so much. The last thing I want is to be the trigger for negative emotions and experiences for him. It feels like a betrayal of his trust in me. He is only four years old. Every time I have to explain to Connor why I must go into hospital again, I feel his body tighten and see that frightened, almost betrayed, look come into his eyes. He says to me, 'Mummy, why do you have to keep leaving me?'

This will be the seventh time in ten months. More away than at home. More instability than stability. He may be reasonably used to it all; we all are. He may put on a brave 'show' – we all do – but I know Connor really hates it. We all really hate it.

I hold out for as long as I possibly can before I will even consider another period of hospitalisation. Only when the pain has become unbearable, the exhaustion overwhelming and the feeling of being terribly ill insurmountable; only then do I agree that it might be best for me, best for all of us, if I return to hospital for yet more treatment.

It's not just tough on me and Connor; it causes disruption and stress for the whole family circle. My husband has to juggle the deadlines of his demanding job with running a house and providing additional emotional and practical support for Connor. He has to fit in visiting and supporting me with talking to doctors and other health professionals. It is hard for his employers to go on being sympathetic when the crisis situations keep recurring.

It's tough for the Grannies too, trying to provide additional security and routine and being there as mother figures for Connor. They are having to deal with early morning starts and childcare demands, at the very point when things should finally be getting easier for them. They are dropping so much of their own lives, just to keep ours ticking by. I am haunted by guilt at the impact my illness and the hospital visits have on the people I love the most. The hardest thing is when someone's immediate response to hearing that I have to go into hospital again is to say, 'Oh poor, poor Connor.' I feel bad enough. I want someone to reassure me that he will be all right.

My hospital stays can last from a couple of days to a few weeks or even months. Once it was for a three-month period. I was extremely ill and it was an unspeakably awful time. The separation from Connor was particularly dreadful as the only way he could cope (aged just under four years) was to shut himself off emotionally from Mummy. The pain was too much for him. On top of everything else that I seemed to have lost at that time (I had suffered something similar to a stroke and had lost the power down my left side and some of my sight) I had to deal with this 'closing down' from the son that I loved so dearly and missed so much. More than anything I missed being there to cuddle him at night. I yearned so very, very much to be his Mummy again. Sometimes during bouts of missing Connor and home sickness I would ring home and find that he wouldn't even talk to me.

Connor's visits to hospital always seemed to be very difficult, no matter how hard we tried. Often there would be new toys or interesting things to do to try and distract Connor away from how very ill I was. I always made a huge effort to be at my best physically and mentally for his visits; often that would be my main focus and goal for the day. But even so, the visits frequently didn't go well. Connor was upset when he came, upset while he was there and upset when he left. But of course he was also upset when he didn't come.

We tried to give Connor regular 'days off'; a break from the exhausting routine of hospital visiting, when he could just putter around at home with a friend. I knew this was good for him, but emotionally I always found it very hard to cope with.

For a long time I was living in a drugged twilight world in which pain was paramount. My husband and I were, naturally, very worried and upset. We tried to protect Connor from the nightmare of what was happening, but it was impossible not to transfer to him some of our anxiety. Connor couldn't understand (and neither could we) why I couldn't see properly, could barely move and had changed in personality and appearance. This wasn't the Mummy he knew. No wonder he retreated into the defence of 'shutting down' and looking to his Daddy to be both parents.

In some ways it was harder still when I began the process of rehabilitation and started to go home regularly for weekends. Connor loved me being back. Gradually over the weekend the closeness of our relationship would start to return. He used to say he wanted me to stay forever and that it didn't matter if I couldn't look after him, as long as I was there for him. I tried to cling on to this affirming and encouraging statement like a beacon of light in the dark but I knew how much Connor dreaded my return to hospital after each weekend. Sundays and Monday mornings were filled with sore tummies and distressed and difficult behaviour.

I remember so vividly an incident that took place at that time. It was a Monday afternoon and Connor had come to visit me in hospital. He started to cry and asked lots of questions. Why did I have to return to hospital? Why couldn't I stay at home for good? Why was I ill? Why did I have to leave him? He was shaking and crying so much it was as if a glacier had started to melt and the tears and pain were flowing out of him with so much more pain still to come. I knew the answers I was giving him were the 'right' ones but they didn't make any real sense to him or me. In the end I started to cry with him, to share our pain together. I cuddled him and we sat, rocking back and forth, still crying together. Some people have criticised me for crying with my son, but I believe that following my gut instinct to share some of our grief together was the only right and real thing to do at that time.

Coming home called for adaptations from all of us. I struggled with the fact that whilst previously Connor would have called out instinctively to me if he was hurt, or needed someone in the night, he now called for his Daddy. Rationally, I could understand that for the past three months he had learned to rely on his father for everything, but it left me feeling displaced. I wanted to be emotionally connected with my son again, even if, practically speaking, there was very little I could do for him as yet.

At the same time, all the anger, frustration, pain and insecurity that had built up inside Connor exploded like a volcano and was directed towards me. Anger, tantrums, hysterics, difficult and disturbed behaviour; raw pain, ending always with the baseline question, 'Mummy why did you leave me? I missed you so much.'

It can be very hard to know how much to tell Connor when I am in a medical crisis. There are times when I have to go and see one of my consultants for an emergency appointment and I know that there is a 50:50 chance that I will have to be admitted to hospital. I don't want to cloud Connor's world or worry him unnecessarily, but I am consumed by the thought of how terrible it would be for him if he went to school one morning and came home to find his Mummy had gone into hospital when he wasn't expecting it.

How does life progress for us? With a hospital suitcase always three-quarters packed, and the thought of being ready for the next hospital trip hovering like a cloud in my mind. I try always to have a suitable supply of ready meals in the freezer for the family to use when I am away and a store of suitable hospital presents for Connor. I am forever gathering up small-size toiletries and collecting change for the hospital phone.

I know that we will always find a way of dealing with the difficulties and yet the pain inside is like a wounding to my innermost being, causing me to gasp for air, emotionally, as the focus and joy of my life is temporarily shifted.

Banality

Rhoda J Olkin

Jenny Kesselman sits on the hard folding chair in the multi-use room at her son's school, a pen poised above the small notebook which is balanced on her knee. She has written: 'There is nothing as banal as a Boy Scout troop meeting', but now she frowns, wondering about the spelling of 'banal'. There is no one sitting next to her, which is not unusual, so she leans over the empty chair and taps the shoulder of the mom two seats down.

'Banal; B-a-n-a-l, now an e, or not?' There is no answer, but this too is not unusual. 'Well, I guess we'll just have to look it up when we get home, won't we?' Jenny turns back to her notebook and inserts an 'e' at the end of 'banal', draws a circle around it, goes back over the circle carefully in the reverse direction, then finally adds a big question mark above it, with the notation 'Spelling?'

The multi-use room is filled with over three hundred parents, most talking in small groups. Dads have video cameras at the ready and mill around the periphery of the two sections of folding chairs. Flags, alternating between the state and boy scout flag, stand erect in wooden holders lining each side of the center aisle. Jenny surmises that the boy scouts constructed the flag stands as one of their projects. A boy scout is always prepared.

Before Jenny has time to continue her writing (she intends to send her review to the local paper) the pack leader makes a request over the microphone, which squawks gratingly until its volume is properly adjusted. She doesn't understand what he's said, something about colors, but it prompts a group of six boys ('third graders' she writes in her notebook) to march down the aisle carrying the American flag. There is a lot of gesturing in formation and about facing, then the flag is inserted into another holder. The crowd, as if they've rehearsed, stands in unison and begins the pledge of allegiance. Jenny, who has remained seated, wipes a tear from her face; she finds the pledge of allegiance very moving.

The phalanx of third graders retreats. Jenny looks at their brown uniforms, and then thinks of the Nazi youth. For just a moment she feels a rush of panic, but remembers to take a deep breath and say the line her doctor has taught her: 'I can choose to ignore this.' This line, this life line, is to help her distinguish what is outside her head and real, and what is inside her head and may or may not be real. The panic passes, but she has the thought that the boy scouts are really a sham organization, that they will seduce her son with lies and ceremony until he turns on her. But Jason would not do this, she thinks. He has been circumcised into her religion, not the one of his Norwegian father. She wants the audience members to know this, that a boy scout is also loyal, and her son will be loyal to her. She leans forward and puts her hand on the shoulder of the blonde woman in front of her.

'My son's Jewish, you know,' Jenny whispers. The blonde woman jumps, startled. She starts to turn toward Jenny, but the woman on her right leans over and whispers something. Neither one looks back at Jenny, but still she knows what they are saying.

'That's right, honey,' Jenny beams, nodding vigorously. 'You just go right on ahead and explain the facts of Mrs Kesselman to her.' She sits back to watch the first skit. She feels a mounting sense of excitement, looking forward to her son's skit, third on the program.

Shortly after Jason was born she'd tried to send him back. It was at his second well-baby check-up, and he was seven weeks old. The nurse weighed him (just over eight pounds, less than a small Thanksgiving turkey), took measurements of his head size, and told Mrs Kesselman she could go ahead and loosely diaper him again, the doctor would be in shortly. When Dr Kung walked in he found Mrs Kesselman squatting on the floor, her naked baby lying on the carpet beneath the arc of where her legs joined. Jason's hand and wrist were inserted into her vagina.

Jenny did not look up. She heard Dr Kung ask her, in the warm sweet sherry voice that had made her choose him as her son's pediatrician, what she was doing.

'I'm sending him back,' she said.

'And why would that be, Mrs Kesselman?' The doctor knelt down in front of her and gently withdrew Jason's hand. She fell back on to the all-purpose carpet.

Didn't he see? Wasn't it obvious? Jason was clearly too small, too fragile to be out in the world. 'He's not ready yet,' she said. 'He needs more time, you know what I'm saying? My water broke too soon.'

'He was only five days early, and his birth weight was normal. He's doing just fine, Mrs Kesselman.'

'No,' she said firmly. 'He can't survive out here.'

'Not alone, of course.' Dr Kung stood up and extended an arm to her, helping her to her feet. 'That's why he needs you.'

So then why did they hospitalize her?

Children's Protective Services came and took the baby until Stephen, her husband, returned five days later from his conference in Europe. No one had called him; Jenny couldn't remember where he was, not even which country. 'You could look it up,' she kept saying, but no one thought to go into her house and look on the yellow magnetic pad stuck to her refrigerator, where his hotel and phone number were.

Stephen first saw the doctor, before coming to her room and sitting on the edge of her bed. He was furious (she'd expected that) but it was with her.

'Aren't you going to sue?' she asked him.

'Sue who?' This rhyme struck Jenny as funny, and she said it out loud a few times, but in whispers so Stephen wouldn't hear.

'Jenny, what's wrong with you? Can't you pay attention?'

'The doctor says it's post-partum psychosis,' she said. 'That's good, isn't it?'

'What's so good about it?'

'The post-partum part.' (She almost started repeating this alliteration, but was able to stop herself.) 'That means it will pass. It's only temporary.'

'No.' Stephen leaned forward and rested his arms on his knees. Even folded in half like that he was big; his six-six frame had been seeming all that much huger to Jenny since Jason was born. 'No,' he said again. 'It will abate, but it will not go away. It will come back, and back, and back.' Jenny wanted to sway to the rhythm of his words. She started to defend herself, but he continued. 'When I met you, you were working. You were a chemist. You were in a good phase, in remission. It hasn't been the same since.'

Stephen declared he'd had enough. He stayed, looking after Jason, until she got out of the hospital. Then he took a job in Norway.

'What kind of man leaves his infant son with a schizophrenic mother? Who's the crazy one here?' Jenny shouted after his departing plane.

After that CPS came to visit her regularly. She got ready for their visits meticulously. One particular visit she was especially prepared. She made sure the kitchen was well stocked with food. She visited a second-hand store to buy Jason a new jumpsuit. While Jason napped she cleaned his room, then fell asleep herself just as he woke up.

'Never you mind,' she whispered to him. 'I can do without my nap. We're ready, aren't we lovey?' She went with him into the living room to wait.

The CPS lady arrived fifteen minutes early, but Jenny was used to that. She knew it was a way of catching her off guard. This was a new lady she hadn't met before, and Jenny extended her hand.

'Please come in. Would you have time for some tea?'

'No, thank you,' responded the lady, who held a

clipboard at her side. 'Perhaps we might have a little look around, if you don't mind.'

Oh, this one is polite, Jenny had to hand it to her. But that didn't fool her for one moment. Polite was just another word for 'in the best interests of the child'. So she took a few deep breaths and led the lady to Jason's room.

'I was just about to change him anyway,' she declared. She was pleased; this would give her a chance to put Jason in his new pink outfit. She cooed at him as she wiped his tiny bottom, being careful to cover him again quickly with a diaper. (He'd peed on the last lady.) When he was dressed she lifted him into her arms and turned around. She was surprised by the expression on the lady's face as she looked at Jason.

'It's new,' Jenny said quickly. 'New to us, anyway. We got it at a second-hand store. We saved a lot of money, you know.' She smoothed the pink ruffle over Jason's backside, pleased with how it fit him, and thought that he looked like pink cotton candy, good enough to eat.

'Pink is a bit...unusual on a boy,' the lady said.

Jenny froze. She saw her mistake immediately, but thought it wasn't so serious. 'It's only adults who care,' she said, trying not to sound defensive. 'Jason doesn't know the difference. As long as he's healthy. And clean. Like his room.' She tried to divert the lady's attention. Jenny saw her looking at the shelf she had installed across one wall of the baby's room. It was lined with stuffed animals from one end to the other. Jenny had at first put them in order of height, but then she remembered that sometimes other people thought behaviours like that were odd, so she grouped them by name, according to her own scheme that no one would know.

But once again the lady frowned. 'Did you arrange them yourself?' she asked.

'Yes.' Jenny decided not to say anything more just yet. This could be a trick question, like the one at the hospital about what you'd do if you noticed a fire breaking out in a crowded theater.

'I can't help but notice how neat they are.'

Jenny relaxed; it was a compliment after all. 'Thank you.'

The lady shot her a strange look. 'They seem to all be facing the same way, their toes pointing in one direction.'

Jenny started to say 'South-west', then realized she had been trapped, after all.

'Hmmm,' was all the lady said, but Jenny knew she was writing words like 'excessive' and 'obsessive' on her form. The lady turned to go into the kitchen, and this time she was in the lead and Jenny was following.

'Perhaps I will have that tea now, after all,' the lady said, sitting at the kitchen table. Jenny smiled; she thought the tea was a really good sign. She put Jason in the bouncer seat on the floor (never on the counter). As she poured the hot water from the Thermos (this, too, she had planned ahead), she hummed softly. This helped remind her not to make small talk, which always seemed larger than it should, and got her in trouble with CPS.

'Earl Grey okay?' (*Grey okay* she repeated to herself.)

'Yes, fine.' The lady was looking at something on the table, Jenny couldn't be sure what. She handed her the mug of tea, and sat down with her own cup in hand.

'Isn't that baby food?' The lady indicated several opened, emptied jars on the single placemat on the table. Next to them was a dirty spoon, but a regular sized one, not the small white plastic-coated one she used for Jason. 'Were *you* eating the baby food?'

For a moment Jenny considered lying, but knew she wouldn't succeed. After the wave of humiliation passed she felt indignant. 'You are here to check on the baby,' she said. 'He is healthy. He is bathed. He is dressed in a fresh outfit and his diaper is changed. He sleeps in a clean room, and he eats well.' Her voice was growing louder and she tried to control it. 'What *I* eat is no one's business.'

'But surely you must understand that eating baby food simply isn't...'

Jenny waited. She knew the next word was 'appropriate'. That was a big word in psychiatry. 'Dress inappropriate to weather. Behavior not appropriate to situation. Affect not appropriate to content.' Once she'd asked her doctor if that was her diagnosis: inappropriate. He'd taken her question seriously.

As the CPS lady was leaving she explained to Jenny that the next visit would not be scheduled. They would be *stopping by* to check on *things*.

Sometimes they left with just their clipboards. Other times they took Jason. But Jenny always got him back. She had a sizeable bank account from her divorce settlement, and she used it for what mattered most. 'I have brains and I have money, and now I have a lawyer,' she said to her doctor. 'I also have schizophrenia, but that is neither here nor there.'

She took her medications daily, and she practiced reality testing. So mostly Jason lived with her. And when he was almost three she started him in preschool at the Jewish Community Center two mornings a week. She kept track of the days on a big calendar in the kitchen, so she didn't forget to take him. (She knew that *continuity* was very important for a child because CPS was always telling her this, sometimes as they were taking him away.) The preschool was a cooperative, and she was expected to help two mornings a month. She liked the *idea* of helping out, but the reality of it made her head hurt. The cacophony was hard for her, it felt like a million voices shouting in her head, and she had to work extra hard to tune them out. Sometimes she tuned out the actual requests from actual children, but this couldn't be helped, she thought. On her fourth time they relieved her of her cooperative duties.

When Jason was four she asked Dr Kung the question that she had been waiting to ask since his birth. She slipped it in between whether she should be concerned that he still wore a diaper at night and if he could survive on only peanut butter sandwiches. 'Is he normal?' she asked.

'He's quite healthy, if that's what you mean,' Dr Kung replied.

'That's not what I mean. He looks just like his father; is

he like his father? Or is he like me?'

'Mrs Kesselman, I won't lie to you. Schizophrenia does run in families, but that only makes it a higher probability compared to the rest of the population. There is simply no way of knowing about any one individual. In Jason's case he is developing well, and there is no way to predict what will happen. It is important to treat him normally, and give him a range of...' he hesitated briefly, '...outside experiences.'

'Outside me, you mean.'

So when he was seven she enrolled him in the Boy Scouts, so he could be with normal boys, and do normal boy stuff. And when he got older he kept his own room clean, and he never wore pink. CPS was pleased, and the ladies came around less often.

Jenny puts her notebook under the folding chair. She doesn't want any distractions as her son's skit begins. She feels she is a beam of halogen light shining across the darkened room toward Jason on the stage, and hopes her brightness will not distract him. Her eyes focus on him, taking in his mad scientist costume, the way his hair stands up at the back of his head, opposite his chin. She sees a small drop of drool begin to fall from his mouth, and she feels drawn in, the feeling like watching a raging stream off a low bridge, a sense of being pulled in by the current. She merges with him as they swim downstream together, two small rivers joined into a mighty stream.

The sound of applause makes the moment pass. The room is no longer shielded in darkness, the lights are brighter now. She can see more clearly. As she looks up at Jason taking his bow on the stage she sees how very banal he is. He fits right in here, with the other boy scouts. She feels an enormous relief. Then with a rush she starts to cry. Her tears fall on to her hands which are resting in her lap. As she looks down at a teardrop she feels that this time she enters the water alone.

There are Worse Things than Being Bored

Beth Weil

I was 39 when I had my cerebral hemorrhage. It was 1991. I was playing with a Bluegrass band called the Good Ol' Persons in Southern California. On the last beat of the last song of the set, a blood vessel burst in my brain. Within ten minutes I was unable to speak or use my right side. I had two operations on my brain that night and was in a coma for three weeks.

When I came to, I was in an air-ambulance going from Southern California to Redwood City, which is in the San Francisco Bay Area. The doctors had removed half of my skull so that the swelling wouldn't kill me. I was unable to sit up, and my right side, including my face and one vocal cord, was paralyzed, so I must have looked and sounded strange to say the least.

As far as my attitude and mental health went I was living utterly in the present; I didn't think about where I had been or what was going to happen in the future. When I was miserable, it would be over something that had just occurred. I was also on a ventilator so that I couldn't talk until I came off it shortly before being transferred to Kaiser Vallejo for rehabilitation. It was there that my kids first saw what had happened to me.

My son, Matt, had just turned five. Even before my bleed his life had been eventful – he had trouble controlling himself and he had been to a number of pre-schools before he was in kindergarten. Matt had to be persuaded to come into the room where I was. He was understandably upset and he didn't know why this had happened to me. My feelings were a little hurt, but I couldn't spend time thinking about it. My speech was minimal – I think I could say little more than 'yes', 'no', 'maybe', and a few phrases – so I couldn't have made him feel better anyway.

My daughter, Rachel, was two and a half, and she didn't understand what had happened either. She was busy showing-off; getting on my bed and cuddling me until she found she wasn't getting very much attention and then running off around the hospital. Even at the age of two, she was her own person; she was in charge, and there was little I could do about it. So I just lay there and let it happen.

When I came home, it was only for five days. Then I had to go down to Redwood City to get my skull replaced. It had been kept on ice, so that if I didn't die they could replace it. When I got home, my kids suddenly switched roles. Matt started to pay attention to me; wanting to know if anything was wrong, and could he do anything? He didn't say these things to me directly but talked through his dad. I suppose he was not able to express his feelings directly because of the unfamiliarity of the situation. It was a few more years before he was able to speak to me about this.

Rachel, on the other hand, became angry. She started to ignore me and depended more and more on her dad. It was as if the 'old' me had died, and been replaced by a 'new' me, who couldn't do nearly as much stuff for her or for myself. I ask her today whether she remembers me before my bleed, and she says she doesn't. So for her I have always been disabled, and that is just part of life. I am saddened by her having no memory of the non-disabled me. She can hear me sing on a record I made before my bleed, and she can see pictures of me as I was then, but that is all.

I was, and still am, amazed by all this. I thought that Matt, being a boy, would be uncomfortable around me, and would show his discomfort by avoiding me. I am happy that this is not the case. I thought that Rachel would help me since we are both female. I thought she would want to be in charge of both herself and me. In some ways this has come to pass, and maybe I should be glad for the self-reliance it gives me when she doesn't take charge. It is like that to this day, six and a half years later – Matt will be more concerned when anything is wrong, and more willing to help. Rachel's anger has subsided somewhat, but it is still there. She knows she has to help me in public restrooms and the like, and sometimes she clearly resents it. When I cry, she doesn't want to be seen with me. 'I don't want to go with a mother that's crying,' she says.

A few years ago a friend asked me how I dealt with the self-image problem, and I said that it wasn't a problem. I couldn't worry about how I defined myself, whilst I was having problems merely staying alive. Later, I could have had difficulties with my new self-image, but I never did. I have always considered myself lucky in that respect. And now I just live one day at a time. I am still paralyzed and have brain damage. The results of having a bleed and a stroke are similar – both can destroy your ability to control tears and your short-term memory. So I remember yesterday and that's about all, until you get into periods of time that happened before my bleed.

I am divorced now and share joint custody of the kids, one week with me, then one week with him. I don't hate my ex-husband, but I do hate the bleed for what it did to us. He has a new wife now, and they have a daughter who is three. Rachel gets to be the big sister and she says that being at my house is boring. I tell her, tough. After all, there are worse things than being bored.

On Being a Hawaiian Auntie

Julia Dolphin Trahan

Rebecca, my older sister, is a widowed mother who lives a block away from my apartment. She gave birth to Kelani, my energetic niece, almost three years ago. My family and I are US mainland transplants but Kelani was born here. In Hawaiian culture the role of 'Auntie' involves tremendous responsibility in giving wise guidance and gentle strength. I can't always live up to these expectations. I do try. I visit Kelani daily to play dinosaurs, swim or munch on cookies.

I had never held a baby until I looked after one-year-old Kelani. I felt intimidated; fearful of looking awkward or dropping the child. The first time I babysat, Kelani began to howl. The only thing I knew about childcare was from magazines: 'If a child cries, pick her up and give her comfort.' I did this immediately and Kelani clung tight and screamed louder. I panicked. Dad finally came in and changed her diaper.

Returning at the end of my visit to my home in San Francisco, I didn't understand my value to Kelani. My parents would tell me, 'Kelani often asks where you are,' so when Kelani wanted nothing to do with me when I saw her again, a month after her second birthday, I was puzzled. I had given up my San Francisco apartment and was living not far from my family in Waikiki, but with no idea of whether I would leave or stay. Of course I had brought family presents, but even then Kelani turned her back on me. One day she was sitting on the kitchen floor, trying to ignore me, but suddenly she turned around and asked, 'Are you leaving again?' Without thinking I said, 'No', and we've been pals ever since.

Kelani asks a lot of questions. Why can't I hold her hand and walk at the same time? Why can I run up some stairs and not others? Why do some stairs have hand-rails and others don't? Why do I need my crutch some times and not others? Why can't I run like Mommy? Why can I do some things with my left arm but not other things? These questions have reasonably straightforward answers, but I wonder how I should explain the questions or stares we get when I am pushing her one-handed and limping in her baby jogger. My worry is that she will become fearful, and pick up judgemental values from strangers or my family. This hasn't been the case so far; her attitude is pretty much, 'That's the way Aunt Julie is.'

For my part I am inspired by Kelani's athleticism and love of using her body. Jumping off the bed or the chair, throwing her feet in the air, and seeking always for new, higher places to stand on, provide hours of entertainment. Watching her try and retry activities and playing an active role in teaching her how to swim have helped me to explore and accept my physical limitations. Her charming showmanship has encouraged me to let people see me try new things. Even as a non-disabled child I used to hide my trials and errors.

With Kelani as my role model I am learning that it is worth facing a bit of self-consciousness to be able to turn early morning somersaults in the warm ocean. I have recently found a calm spot with fairly firm sand where I can get in and out of the water independently, using my crutch – my toy, as Kelani calls it. Whilst I swim I leave it wedged between the rocks, about 50 feet off shore. Swimming towards the beach I look back at the bluish green metal pole, tiny and proud against the rocks and the vast expanse of the ocean.

I have a 'warrior princess' doll that Kelani identifies with me because Angela, the doll, carries a plastic sword and I have a sword tattoo. She also carries a staff. I tell Kelani about how Angela needs her staff to walk with. It is helpful to be able to explain things to Kelani by building a story around the doll. And I don't mind being a warrior princess for a couple of hours...

Reflections of a Mama Bear

Sylvia Dick Gomez

They line up
on the schoolyard
to take turns.
'It's my go, Marjorie!'
'No Ben, you went yesterday.
Today is Jesse.'
A small general,
she maintains order among the troops,
decides which soldier shall mount the cavalry
of my scooter
and weave between the trees
before returning triumphant
to the castle.

'I'm so lucky,'
she confides.
'My Mommy's accessible.'

At the edge of a pool,
the wheelchair is a rock
upon which the Queen of the Mermaids
rests
after diving for pearls
with her Little Mermaid.
She offers instruction
in the finer points
of undersea etiquette.

Who cares
if the Queen flounders?
That's what mermaids do.

In the shadows
among the trees,
the chair
is a Wise Women's Lodge,
from which she emerges
on very special occasions
to lie on the earth
with other members of her tribe
and count a million stars.

Together
we fly
among the stars.

So,
when you pat my scooter
and observe grimly,
'It must be hard for her to see you like this,'
I say nothing.
Later,
as we zoom down the street
singing,
I glance at our storefront reflection.
'Look, Baby, what do you see?'

'You are the eagle,'
she replies.
'and I am the little bird sitting on your shoulders!

You are the space ship
and I am the astronaut!
You are the Mama Bear
taking her baby bear home.'

And that night,
when Mama Bear and Sister Bear
bed down for a long hibernation
in the safety of their cave,
I am thankful, oh so very thankful,
that in this great big world,
one small person
sees me as I am.

Part IV
Home

In My Mind's Eye: IV
Raising Peter

Jo Litwinowicz

As Peter grew bigger, our one-bedroom bungalow was over-run with toys, clothes and other things. Everywhere I turned I ran over or broke his toys. I was at my wit's end. I couldn't feed Peter properly when he started on solids because there wasn't room in the kitchen to put him in his high chair. Feeding Peter was a bit hit and miss anyway as he wouldn't keep still and, with the tremor in my hand, food didn't always end up in his mouth but on the carpet or on the settee.

I had put our name down to be rehoused when I knew I was pregnant. I asked if we could have a house by the park where all the young families lived, so that Peter would have friends to play with. There were no children where we were and people liked it quiet. Also to get to our bungalow you had to cross a main road and mums wouldn't walk up a steep hill to see us. But I was told there was no possible way we could move down there as we needed a bungalow specially designed for a wheelchair.

I made friends with a woman who lived up the road with her elderly parents. She had to keep her daughter, who was a month younger than Peter, strapped in a pram as her parents wouldn't allow the little girl to play all over the house. So she came down to see me in the mornings and the children could play and keep each other company. When the woman got a part-time job she left her daughter with me three mornings a week for two hours, which was great. While the children played I could get on with my chores and prepare lunch, plus Peter ate better when there was a friend with him.

Things were less stressful for me now and I managed to

relax more, making Peter less tense. I tried taking him out in a sling as I was frightened of him slipping off my lap when I was going down the hill in my wheelchair. I had somehow to propel my wheelchair with one hand and keep on an even keel, but the sling was difficult to manage and Peter hated to be tied in. People used to say, 'Your problems will really start when Peter begins to walk. You won't be able to catch him.' But when he started walking at eleven months, it was as if someone had opened a window for me and for him too. By the time he was one year old he was running, so I got some reins and taught him to walk up and down our little road with his arm on my left armrest till I was confident he would be safe walking alongside me on the road.

When Peter was two my husband got me a battery car and made a seat for Peter to sit next to me so I didn't have to struggle up and down the hill in my manual wheelchair. Peter loved it and nicknamed my buggy 'Moby Dick'. The name stuck even when I changed it for a newer model.

Eventually someone moved and left a two-bedroomed bungalow free, but after we moved there, it was difficult getting Peter to sleep in his own room by himself; it took us a year to manage it. My parents and my brother came up to see us about five times a year. Peter adored his uncle Les, and he still worships him. My parents, however, continued to think that Peter would be better off living with them, and at every opportunity they made me cry and feel a fool in front of my son. I got used to it in time and it didn't bother me, but I regret not being able to share my pleasure with my mother. I imagined us shopping for baby clothes; doing things together. I never could do anything right in their eyes and I wasted a lot of time and energy trying to get their blessing.

When Peter was five we took him for the first time to stay with my parents. We went for picnics, to the zoo and so on, but one day Peter went quiet and I said, 'What's up Peter?' He said he was okay but he was quiet all evening. I knew that he would tell me when he was ready. Anyway at bedtime he said, 'Mum, when I get older I'll live here.'

I said, 'Do you like it here?' He shook his head saying, 'Not really, but do you notice how everyone in this town is like me and where we live a lot of people are like you?' It was the first time he'd mentioned my disability and I was relieved in a way as it made me feel he accepted me as I am. It was the same way I felt when I was growing up, but in reverse – if I saw a disabled child I used to think, 'Oh, that person's like me.'

I made up my mind that as soon as we got back I'd make sure he mixed more outside the village. I wrote to the Spastics Society and to a lot of disabled holiday places explaining that I wanted a family holiday, but no organisation was willing to take Peter and me together. They all wrote back and said that seeing my son was able-bodied he could not come at the same time. I wrote to Pontins asking if they had chalets for wheelchairs and they said their access was fine so when Peter was nine he and I went on holiday. It was a nightmare for me, I couldn't get into the loo or have a shower. I had to take my chair to the other side of the camp to charge it and the place was locked from 6 p.m. to 11 a.m. the next day so I was without my electric chair for over 12 hours. Using my manual chair was exhausting but I wasn't going to rely on Peter as it was his holiday and he enjoyed it.

While Peter was growing up I managed to take him on holiday just twice. It was hard for me to accept, as Peter missed out on a lot. When I was growing up the Spastics Society would take me on trips and holidays, but there was no back-up to help disabled people take their able-bodied kids out, especially if the parents had no transport of their own.

I contacted the Children's Society to see if they could help. A nice woman came and told us about their 'Befriending Scheme'. She said that usually they helped children who came from broken homes. She told me, 'As yet you are the first disabled person who has asked if there's a chance of us taking your son for a few hours a week to mix with different people.' They hadn't thought about the needs of disabled parents and their children but they were willing to try.

A couple were sent by the scheme to meet us and they were lovely people. Peter took to them straight away. They came from a village eight or nine miles away. The lady ran a bed and breakfast and they had a huge garden plus two cats, two dogs, two horses and two sheep which appealed to Peter as we couldn't have pets due to my husband's allergies. Peter loved going there. They took him on country walks, showing him things on the way and explaining what they were. They took him swimming and he helped them with gardening and he also helped build a car. When he was nine they had other children staying for a week in the summer holidays and asked him too.

They were lovely to Peter but unfortunately the man died of cancer when Peter was 12, which broke his heart, though we still see the woman now and again. I contacted an organisation called Crossroads who sent a volunteer called Pat, who has become part of the family now. We have been ice-skating, bowling, and we have weekend trips to London and go for birthday meals together. We go Christmas shopping and to fairs and just to see Peter's face light up is all the thanks I've ever needed.

Now Peter is 15 he has his own life and he doesn't need me so much, which I'm pleased about. If I hadn't fought to have him but had done what everyone told me to do, I wouldn't have all the love and joy that Peter brought with him into this dull world of mine, making it into a wonderful colourful world. As yet I have not heard the words 'I don't want a mum that's in a wheelchair' as that woman from the Family Planning clinic told me he would say. But he did say words that brought tears to my eyes. When he was 14 we were talking about marriage and I said, 'When you buy a house make sure I can get in,' and he said, 'I might buy a bungalow somewhere.' I said, 'That's nice, thinking of your mum,' and he said, 'I wasn't. The girl I fall in love with might be in a wheelchair.' Well, you could have knocked me down with a feather!

Enmeshed

Vicky D'aoust

My daughter and I are both Deaf[1] and we are both single, in that she has no siblings and I am not married or in a relationship. Perhaps because of this, and at least in part due to our choice, we bonded very closely from the outset. We were what some psychologists call 'enmeshed'.

I was already a fluent signer when I adopted Marianne and so, from the day I met her (at which point she was three years old) up to the current time, we have always been able to express how we feel to each other. This can be difficult in families where sign language is not common to both parent and child.

Many times Marianne has accused me of being too much part of the English-speaking culture because I spell out or initialize a sign and I feel a bit ashamed or guilty for not being a pure enough model for her. Our language skills are so much better in sign language than in English, because English is very much a second language for her. We can barely communicate over the tele-text phone, or even using e-mail.

Because I lost my hearing and was not born deaf I have always been a marginal member of the Deaf community, whereas she is a full member. However, having a Deaf mother (or in my case deafened) also gives her special status and she is the envy of many of her friends.

When she arrives home my daughter opens her arms, not only for hugs but to tell me all about her week and what she wants to do on the weekend. Our signs are not odd, or 'special' or cute as hearing people often perceive

---

[1] The author has chosen to use 'deaf' (lower case) to describe one who cannot hear, whereas 'Deaf' (upper case) refers to the self-defined cultural identity that many deaf people share, with pride.

them to be (and too often choose to share with me); for us it is our natural form of communication. We chat about TV, about sex, about school work and we exchange looks and roll our eyes in public, knowing with a fair degree of certainty that no one else understands what we are saying. It can feel as though we are teenagers using codes to talk about secrets.

When Marianne was eight I began to have some health problems associated with my deafness. I was dizzy, nauseous and had fallen more than a few times. As I got more ill, I also became depressed. Within a few months I had lost 40 pounds and was starting really to neglect my daughter. It was obvious to everyone that I needed help. The doctor finally arranged for me to be hospitalized and Marianne was placed into temporary foster care, with a 'mother' who could sign and a 'father' who was Deaf, in a home that had several other foster children. I visited them twice on 'passes' out from the hospital and I am sure Marianne was well cared for, but that didn't change the feeling I had in the pit of my stomach – that I had failed as a mother. Emotionally it shook me so badly that I couldn't sit in any public place without weeping. Just the sight of a family, or even a child with an adult, made me cry.

As I was recovering, and my strength began to come back, I felt ready and able to mother again. However, when I tried to arrange this I was met with resistance; the foster care authorities did not want to return my daughter to me yet. They said they did not think I was ready and that I might have to go back to the hospital; they would rather Marianne (who knew nothing of this) was not bounced around. I was stunned. I have a progressive disorder that is not going to get any better and they were saying that I was not ready!

I panicked. I went through my emotional closet to decide which reaction to use. I thought of anger, revenge, depression and even denial but the response that seemed to fit best was – flee. Although it took more than a month to orchestrate, I packed up and moved out of the jurisdiction, and took my daughter with me.

We arrived in our new home, where I was determined to be healthy. I found a fantastic little private school within walking distance from the house that had both deaf and hearing students. It provided the support my daughter needed, other parents were wonderful and some of my Deaf friends lived nearby. I was on a roll.

But within three months of settling in I was in hospital again, this time for an unknown allergic reaction. The impact this had on my daughter was far worse than before. She witnessed me turning red and then blue, as I stopped breathing. I was rescued, and survived, but she was traumatized. Luckily, this time, I had supportive friends who took care of her. However, the allergic reactions came frequently and the doctors had a very hard time identifying the cause. My asthma grew worse and eventually I had a respiratory arrest and brain hemorrhage which resulted in physical disabilities. I awoke from the unconscious state unable to see properly, unable to walk, in fact barely able to breathe. After five weeks of rehabilitation I was returned home using a wheelchair and eating puréed foods. I was given 20 hours of home care per week.

When I arrived home my daughter referred to me as the 'new mom'. She constantly asked where the old mom had gone. My daughter was a really good sport though, she cried very seldom and supported me like an adult might support an older person – with care and respect. She showed maturity beyond her years and a great deal of patience. She watched a lot of TV during this time, and I slept a lot. We had friends and her regular school activities gave her lots of social time, but I had changed. I didn't play ball with her, I didn't cook for her and I couldn't go to the corner store. We had homemakers to do the shopping and cleaning. I was dependent on the home-makers and so, indirectly, was Marianne.

Marianne got used to this, but in a negative way. In a few years, by the time I had really regained my independence, she was no longer 'mother's little helper'. Now she wanted 'those women' to do it. When I asked her to do the laundry she said, 'No. Wait for the helper to do it.'

Marianne and I changed mid-motherhood. During the two years that I was very sick, she had to be cared for by other adults, some who loved her and some who were paid to care for her. During those years I had less of my time available, mainly because I was sleeping so much but also because I was emotionally very fragile. I cried really easily and was not much fun to be with. I would be healthier and regaining strength, only to have another allergic reaction and a return to hospital. Marianne saw me as unstable.

But there were also good times. When I was well enough, I would go out on my three wheeled scooter. I was the star of the neighborhood zooming around in my new vehicle. I couldn't think of the right verb to describe it; it wasn't really driving and it wasn't pushing or operating, so Marianne and I called it zooming. Sometimes Marianne would zoom too, either sitting on my lap, standing on the back or on a skateboard behind me. This was cool.

However I was always nervous because of the possibility of having an allergic reaction. The fear alone had kept me in the house for a year. I was more controlled in my house, more able to screen out bad things. At first, Marianne was ever vigilant – checking all the food I was eating, making sure I didn't eat food which might have contained something I was allergic to. I am even triggered by scents, strong fragrances, bleaches and gases, so she would walk ahead of me and smell the air and warn me of upcoming danger.

But Marianne became angry at the restrictions that my allergies posed. At 12 she came home wearing perfume, and at 13 started spraying deodorizing products in the bathroom. She was angry and was acting out. We had fights about how serious my allergies were and how she could be making them worse. She argued about wanting freedom and said that I had medicine I could take. We sometimes had fights that ended in violence, with her hitting me and me restraining her, but she was far stronger than me so I was often afraid. We usually made up quickly after these fights, but they came often enough to keep me on edge. She started smoking, as many teenagers do, and we argued about that. I warned her of the health risk and reminded her that she could never smoke around me. We argued about anything and everything. All the while I was reading and researching adolescence and talking to other mothers. I knew I was not alone, but I still worried about my daughter.

What has made our situation different, or unique perhaps, is that because we are Deaf we are far more restricted in who we can turn to for help. She has only two friends in the local area who can sign, all her other friends live miles and miles away throughout the province. I have a few friends who I communicate with but I don't want to use 'friends' as therapists, I want them as support. So we had a lot of trouble trying to find a therapist and counsellor who would be able to communicate with both Marianne and me and who would also understand my disability. We did eventually find someone and used her for a while but Marianne and I started fighting about that too and I felt that it was one of many topics of argument that we could do without. So we agreed to stop seeing the therapist and to try to be nice to each other. We made a deal that if things ever got really bad, then we would go back to the therapist. Surprisingly, and to my delight, since that agreement, we have not had any major confrontations. It has improved, although the memories are still fresh.

My daughter is growing up and I am proud to see her emerging into a strong young Deaf woman, secure in her Deafness and confident of her identity. I am also proud of how Deaf she is, how capital D deaf my daughter has turned out to be. I know that we had a rough time, and that it was not easy for her. I am also aware that it gave her skills she will use over and over again in her future. I am hopeful that the skills I gained will also come in handy as we eventually separate and she becomes an independent woman.

The Devil's Confusion

Jodi Hoar

There's a piece of dialogue in Toni Morrison's book *Beloved*. It goes:

'You looking good.'

'Devil's confusion. He lets me look good long as I feel bad.'

As a woman with hidden disabilities I know that more than anything, this confusion has come to dominate my life. How is it that I can be in so much pain and feel so tired when no one seems to be able to identify why I am sick let alone provide a cure? And how is it that I can feel so bad without looking sick or disabled?

I was one of those people who managed to live my life with all of the invincibility of a teenager right into my twenties. I lived hard and fast, I played hard and fast and I worked hard and fast. At one point, when my son was still a toddler, I held down three jobs, juggling everything but enough sleep for myself.

And then, eight years ago, I got sick. It sounds so inadequate to say those words because I didn't just get sick. I didn't just get a cold or virus or flu that laid me up for a couple of weeks. What I 'got', or what happened then, is still the source of a lot of medical speculation and personal reflection which I can only describe as feeling as if I'd been cast adrift.

In the beginning, the diagnosis was mononucleosis – a virus that makes you feel as though your body is being crushed by gravity while giving you a sore throat and very swollen lymph glands, liver and spleen. Usually it runs its course in two to four months; except that I didn't get better. And as my condition baffled specialist after specialist, nothing seemed clear except that my elevated white blood cell count indicated some kind of infection; but what kind, no one could say. I had sore throats, swollen glands, muscle aches and *fatigue* until I felt as if even my soul had been permeated by its presence. At times I felt I had been both cursed by some Unknown and abandoned by the medical profession. And so in this confusion, the metaphor of being cast adrift seems a much better way of expressing what happened than saying, eight years ago I got sick.

Now being sick obviously poses a number of problems for single parents and in the beginning I problem-solved the same way anyone would. I enlisted friends and neighbors to help with the general upkeep of my house, the transportation of my kids to school and the running of errands. But it only seemed possible to enlist others for a limited amount of time, and eventually I could not in good conscience ask for any more favors because it seemed more and more unlikely that I would ever be able to return them.

As the weeks and months peeled off into the first year and second year of being sick, the cost to my children was not yet obvious. In fact, by the third year I had regained enough energy to return to work, and I figured that now the sickness was behind us we could have a more active life together. I could finally teach my son to play ball and ride his bike.

You see, my youngest son, who is now 11, was three when it all started. And truth be told I have not picked him up since then. Now as I watch him I can't help wondering how all those years of not being picked up, or roughhoused with, have helped create the young boy who doesn't play any sports. I find myself feeling guilty that I never did teach him to catch a ball or skate. I did manage to teach him to ride his bike, but after the last bout of sickness I cannot ride with him anymore. And that clearly makes him sad.

On the other hand, my daughter is just a couple of years older and there are many shared memories of activities that we both retell. One in particular originally signified nothing more than a funny error in judgement that most adults make at least once. It was her fifth Christmas and I was tossing her in the air, and spinning her around. Unbeknownst to me she had just consumed nearly a liter of chocolate milk. Of course she got sick, and of course she got sick all over me. She still takes great glee in telling that story, but for me it has taken on another, less joyful, meaning. That event stands in my memory as the last time I ever picked up either of my kids and physically played with them.

At the time, of course, it was just an unravelling of time: one day of being tired, but not quite too tired, to play; another day of being too tired to carry anything or either of them, until the tiredness and pain engulfed the rest of their childhood. That's kind of what I mean by being cast adrift. I look back now and I can see them from afar; younger, beckoning, waiting. But my invisible sickness makes it impossible to join them.

It hasn't just been missing out on playing with them. As my disease has progressed, leaving me with less strength and increasing pain, my physical needs have transcended any notion of playing with them into the necessity of designating more and more work onto their shoulders. They have had to pick up the slack, doing the things I no longer even attempt. My son does the groceries. He has an eye for specials and bargains and prides himself on being able to carry them home and save us money. Saving money, making do with very little money, the poverty that accompanies being disabled, is second only in problematics to the array of medical specialists who parade hopes and desolation in front of us.

Even so, I am amazed at how the long-term effects of the poverty that my children have had to become accustomed to, have yet to crystallize into anything but mild disappointments and occasional temper tantrums. Somehow we have managed to make it a winning game to be frugal. We have managed to stand outside of any clear sense that it's not a game we have chosen; it's a necessity for our survival.

My daughter has picked up doing the laundry and some of the cooking. I can no longer lift anything even remotely heavy. Carrying a basket of laundry down to the laundry room will leave me shaking and exhausted for an hour. I try to do the rest of the housework but I wonder about my need to maintain these duties as my own. You see, as I have learned to manage chronic fatigue syndrome, fibromyalgia, arthritis and asthma I have dug in my heels on keeping my house clean, even though this costs me so dearly.

It is ironic that the art of handling the confusions and limitations thrown up by my illness has to a great extent manifested itself as a battle to maintain able-ist notions – by keeping a clean house and not letting my children's lives drift too far from my own, thus perpetuating a contradictory veil not just to those outside of our family but to the kids as well. Even as I explain to them that I am unwell I also take great pains to hide as many of my limitations from them as I can. Only when it reaches the point where I absolutely cannot continue to do something do we discuss it and try to find ways around it.

It seems to me that often in the past, as physical barriers were approached but not yet identified, my children sensed that something was wrong, and felt in their confusion that it was them, or something they were doing, or something they *should* be doing. They may even have had vague anxieties that I was going to die. Their anger has yet to manifest itself; their resentment against a sickness that neither goes away, kills me, nor disfigures me, their bitterness at my never having any extra cash to give them, their incomprehension of an illness that remains invisible and yet is so debilitating.

We all feel it, but how can we discuss these things that confuse us so much? And I know that part of my hesitation has always been to do with hoping and wishing. Hoping that one miraculous day the fog will clear and this invisible veil will lift. For even as I watch my muscle mass shrink, I find myself entertaining notions of a long-term remission or cure, because I can't help feeling that I/we have been randomly and wrongly chosen for some kind of weird revenge and I will shortly be cured, excused, forgiven and freed. And so I hesitate. I hesitate and protect them from knowing about all of my disabilities, about how terrible I feel inside.

And yet, as time passes, more and more I question how my need to hope and wish in this way ultimately denies my own complicity in the confusion. The negotiations and renegotiations between the children and myself are wearing thin. Their benevolence has been stretched to the limit because they still cannot *see* any of my disabilities. The tolerance and faith of children who give parents the authority to say what can and cannot be done, and by whom, is finally being challenged by my children who want things, some things at least, to change *now*.

In this way, and with these dilemmas, we are entering their teen years. The years that for other families bring adolescent challenges to authority and the shirking of duties and responsibilities. But it will be different for us. Other parents can afford to pick up the slack, whereas I cannot. What kind of life will we have without any opportunity for flexibility? What kind of adults are they becoming?

This transition from being 'sick' to being cast adrift in a sea of confusion has alienated me from them and, perhaps worse still, has blocked us from developing an understanding of what it means to be disabled and what that has cost us as a family. Somehow I will have to navigate and explain that many of my demands are not typical, reasonable demands made by me as a parent trying to teach them to be responsible adults, but those of a person struggling not to think of herself as disabled.

My reluctance to accept the disability label, my resistance to talking about the ongoing blending of parental expectations with the needs of a disabled person, is unfair to both them and me. Our energy might be better spent coming to terms with this unique and formative reality rather than dreaming about a different one.

Single Parenthood in 1950s New Zealand

Karen Peterson Butterworth

In 1958, I was accepted for training at Auckland Teachers' College. On my application I told them no lies, although I was stingy with the truth. The medical form asked if I had any serious diseases and I decided not to define polio as serious. I used to pass as 'normal'. Both my legs were equally weak so I did not limp noticeably and, at that time, 'passing' seemed the only route to full social and career acceptance.

Two years later, I conceived my son. It was still a time of strict sexual morality and, like most of my contemporaries, I believed in virginity until marriage. But my sexual urges became too strong for me, the Easter holiday came along and my boyfriend and I spent happy, leisurely hours together in my student flat. Unfortunately, he was on the rebound from a girl with whom he had just broken up and they were quickly reconciled. They were engaged before I confirmed my pregnancy.

My maternal instincts had been awoken early and strongly. My mother used to sit me in the armchair and place my younger siblings in my arms. Holding and feeding them was the main way I could help her in the first years after I had polio. So the emotional pull to keep my baby was overwhelming.

I never seriously considered an abortion, which was illegal and dangerous in New Zealand at that time. While I agonised over what to do, I carried on with my studies. Then one day I fainted in class, and foolishly admitted the reason. The result was instant dismissal, though I was told I could re-enrol after I'd had the baby adopted.

I was two months pregnant when I had to leave college

and my flat. With no money coming in and no social welfare benefit then available, my choices were to go home or to seek shelter with a charitable organisation. My parents lived in a tiny village where the scandal would have been intolerable, so I arranged an interview with a Salvation Army captain who told me, in a kindly manner, that only selfish girls kept their babies. She was sure I was a good Christian girl and that my baby would make some couple very happy.

I then tried an organisation called Motherhood of Man, whose members employed pregnant girls as live-in child-minders. I went to see their social worker who was the first person in authority who really listened to me. She said, 'Well it's plain you want to keep your baby. Let's work out how.' When I had recovered from my tears of relief we worked out a plan of action, but I didn't tell her about my polio. I thought that would stretch her tolerance too far.

I did tell my GP though who, after testing my abdominal and breathing muscles, forecast a difficult birth. He prescribed a surgical corset, which I wore in Auckland's sticky summer heat, and he gave me diaphragm strengthening exercises.

I went to stay with a Motherhood of Man family, where I found the childminding and light household work within my physical capacity. But they treated me like an object of charity, as a lower class of being. When my waters broke I leaped out of bed and, inadvertently, but to my secret satisfaction, ruined my hostess's expensive mat. I took a taxi to the maternity hospital and resolved never to return.

After a long labour I had a high forceps delivery and was advised not to have any more children. But my son was beautiful and we bonded joyfully. I called him Paul after the singer Paul Robeson who had just visited Auckland.

I then took what turned out to be an unsuitable and exhausting live-in job. I stuck it out until Paul was three months old, when a couple of my Wellington friends offered me a room in their large flat. I arranged to resume my teacher training, not telling the college that I had kept my baby. They found out later, but allowed me to stay provided I changed my name by deed poll to give an appearance of marriage.

My college regime left me exhausted. When I pushed Paul's pram through the door after picking him up from his childminder, I just wanted to flop on the bed. But I always made an effort to play with him and I knew I could rest later when he was fed and in bed.

The day Paul discovered that I couldn't run after him was exasperating, but funny too. He would make a game of running away, letting me nearly catch up and then running away again. I quickly learned ways of controlling him verbally, some of them ethical and others pure bribery, like the promise of an ice-cream. I hated doing this but had no other option when he was out of my range and about to go under a car. I would love to know if other disabled mothers have found better ways of managing this situation.

When Paul was five years old, I shifted house in a single weekend. I scrubbed my old flat, packed, and carried and unpacked numerous cartons while the van driver shifted furniture. I fell into bed on Sunday night and on Monday morning I lacked the muscle power to get up.

Paul got his own breakfast, following my instructions, and left for school. Within a few hours I could move enough to take a taxi to see a doctor. When he heard I was a single mother he concluded I had nervous exhaustion and prescribed me Valium without performing any physical examination. When I reached home I phoned a medical student friend, who told me that Valium is a muscle relaxant and that it would make me even weaker. I flushed it down the toilet.

Because the doctor wouldn't write me a medical certificate, I returned to the classroom the next day. But after one day of trying to teach, I needed to take a week's leave and was dismissed.

For the next three years I worked at home, coaching

slow readers and taking in ironing. It was hard financially, but easier physically as I had control over my working environment and could rest whenever necessary. Better still, I was at home enjoying my son.

When Paul was eight I borrowed some money and finished my Bachelor of Arts degree. I then began a full-time career in the public service, which lasted for 20 years. During that time I met the man I later married. He and Paul had initial adjustment problems but he was patient and now they are excellent friends.

My years of struggle have been more than fulfilled as I contemplate my son's confident, kind character. He has a good career, a happy stable relationship and a baby son of his own.

The first two times I saw James he was asleep. It was two weeks, though it seemed an eternity, before Paul and his partner sat me on their sofa with a cushion under my left arm and placed a wide-awake James in my arms. I felt the same awe I had at my own son's smallness, liveliness and helplessness when he was first born.

As I watch my grandson crawl, toddle and walk, I hope that nothing like polio will happen to him. That's a natural wish, we all want to protect our children, yet we know that everyone grows up with losses and most of us survive and learn from them.

I now have post-polio syndrome. I can no longer pass as 'normal', with my splint and my walking stick, but I don't mind any more. My years of pushing against the fatigue barrier probably helped bring on the syndrome, but I would not have missed them for anything. They matured me and enriched my life – and nothing can take that away from me.

Great Mum

Frances Brown

I never planned to be married and have kids. When I was young and at school, my mum was told I'd never be able to have them. Everyone said I wouldn't be able to cope, because I have learning difficulties. My mum only told me this when I left school. She thought if the social worker thought this, it must be right. It made me angry and upset. I never hurt anyone.

Bringing up my son has been wonderful – feeding him, playing, watching him smile and use his fingers to do things makes me really happy. When I have a bad day, and I feel down, I get angry. Then my son cries, I cry and we all end up crying together... It's just hell sometimes!

I have lots of help from my advocate, my sister-in law, a family aide and the Special Parenting Service in Truro. They helped me keep my son. They taught me lots and were there when I needed them.

I dream that my son will be able to grow up and get on with it. I want him to know we are there for him, but he must make his own decisions. I don't want more children; my life is full caring for my son. I am a housewife and problems with my back mean I probably will never work, but I am just happy being a mum.

A Remarkable Woman

Philippa Armstrong

As my 13-year-old daughter snuggled up to me on the sofa, she repeated the description she had heard of me whilst holidaying in Spain with friends, 'She's a remarkable woman.' We giggled softly together and in that moment she, on the threshold of puberty, and I, on the threshold of middle age, expressed our shared experiences, our shared understandings. All the complexities and contradictions contained within that statement were understood.

It is remarkable to be a woman, to have the emotions and body of a woman, to hold within you the magic of life, to carry and to nurture children, to care as women care every day in a paternalistic, often misogynistic society. But we both knew that this was not the only meaning within that statement. I sensed that I was described as a remarkable woman because I have an impairment. All the landmarks of womanhood are masked by perceptions of me first and foremost as disabled, an almost genderless other. Remarkable for simply being a disabled woman.

In that moment, as we giggled together, gone were the ghosts of living with a man who forbade me to mention the difficulties I was having in case it put the insurance up. Who took me to the doctors to get stronger medication when what I really needed was a cleaner. Who wouldn't change a nappy when my hands were so swollen they caused me to cry. Who, in his divorce affidavit, cited that I would be in a wheelchair within 15 years, implying that it would be the worst possible thing that could happen to a parent. And gone was the man who sought custody of the children in order to control me, to make me cook his supper and warm his bed. Who has not been heard of since.

Gone were the ghosts of having to perform in front of the social worker to prove my ability as a parent for fear of losing my children. Gone were the teachers' assertions that my child's reluctance to participate in the field trip was because of 'not wanting to leave you alone because you are disabled', regardless of regular sleep-overs elsewhere, of growing individualism or the possibility that the field trip might even be considered naff.

Gone were the ghosts of invasive surgery, of not really being me, of being reconstructed to conform, of being drugged into another reality, of not being able to access services or benefits unless I was prepared to cooperate with the medical regime.

Gone were the ghosts of being told in my own living room by my local councillor that she would not have had children if she had been me, that she would not have taken the risk of passing on something so terrible, or of burdening the children. Gone were the ghosts of the social services refusing me support on the grounds that 'you have children to help you', of the ordeal for my children of trying to access help because my word on their behalf meant nothing. Of where this placed me in my children's eyes.

In that moment as we snuggled together on the sofa, 'She's a remarkable woman,' my daughter repeated. We giggled, and all the pain melted away.

I Won't Go to Weddings

Shallo Chand

It was the auntyjis; the ones who probe, at no matter what cost, because they feel they have a right to know your personal business. I knew the questions off by heart as these larger than life women peered over me, then buried my head in their big, friendly, suffocating bosoms, with Buddha-like bellies proudly exposed above their saris and hugs that seemed to go on forever.

Why did they need to know? Because. Keeping the tradition going; butting their noses in where they aren't needed...certainly not wanted. 'Never mind, beti. You must have done something dreadful in your last life' – meaning that is why I'm disabled; 'this is the Guru's doing.' How does she know? Did He have a private word? If so, what's He doing discussing my life – hasn't He come across the concept of confidentiality? It was a good way for them to spice up their lives, in between making huge pots of curry and working down at the local rag trade factories. 'Hello beti, how are you coping these days? Are you not better yet? Haven't the doctors found a cure?' I'd smile and not even bother wasting my breath to answer.

Another bullet would be fired...MARRIAGE? When? And to whom? Didn't they ever get bored with my evasive replies? Their only concern was that as a woman, I should be married and have children. It was irrelevant to them that I was disabled; some understanding man from India would make a good suitor for me.

Interestingly, my community never thought disability would be a hindrance. They assumed I would have children and, to my knowledge anyway, never questioned whether it was a practical possibility. I suppose that it was quite a refreshing attitude in a way, compared to being called 'poor thing' or being assumed to be asexual, as my non-Asian peers frequently were, but it was all so loaded. Somehow I couldn't quite reel it in; what lay behind their thinking was far too scary.

In my younger years I felt fearful every time the word marriage cropped up. It carried with it a host of hidden meanings and connotations. It was synonymous with having children to continue the family line and have people to look after you in old age – your very own social service. Procreation was the main and, as far as I could see, the only purpose of marriage. I desperately feared having to live my mother's life, history repeating itself; my own children struggling to appease a father who might turn out to be manipulative and bullying, as mine had been.

My parents were more subtle than the auntyjis; perhaps they recognised the rebel in me even before I saw it in myself. But during weekend visits home from residential college I felt like a caged bird. It wasn't me. I would clam up and dutifully handwash the family clothes, clean the kitchen, help mum to cook; all the preparation that a girl needs in order to make a good wife.

At the age of 18 I got away. I bought a suitcase for £7 and hid it under a pile of stock in the dark corner of the attic, until the chance came. One day mum and dad received a call to say that someone had died and they had to rush to the mourning house for the wailing session. I seized my opportunity and rang for a taxi to take me to the railway station. The suitcase was already in the car but my younger brothers and sisters were begging me not to go. There were floods of tears and uncontrollable sobs but there was no choice; I would never have the courage to do it again, it had to be now. I disappeared to a place I'd never been to; hardly even heard of.

For a couple of years, no one found out where I was, but one day my parents turned up out of the blue. After that there were meetings at weekends. The kids informed me that relatives had been told I was away studying and couldn't come home for a while. I hid behind the myth; it was easier that way.

I was supposedly forgiven, but certainly not forgotten. A year later my father raised the question of an arranged marriage. My suitor was a distant relative, a Punjabi farmer who spoke no English. We would live with my wealthy uncle in Forest Gate and I would work for him for £50 a week. There would be cleaning, cooking and children. Basically, a life like my mum's. After my parents found out that it was me who wrote to the immigration department at the Home Office telling them not to admit my suitor under *any* circumstances, my father didn't speak to me for five years.

Then there was the proposed trip to India. One night in the attic my sister told me she had overheard mum and dad talking about marrying me off in India: 'They're not planning to bring you home.' It was the only way of sorting me out and saving Ijath, the family honour. By this time I had a partner (although my parents did not know this), a job, a life of my own. I told my parents that work commitments would prevent me from making the trip.

Over the years the subject of marriage slowly faded, much to my relief. I refused to go to any weddings, except those of my immediate brothers or sisters. That way I eluded the auntyjis' interrogations and, having no fuel to feed their fires, they left me to get on with my life.

Disability provided a kind of shield for my independence. Within my family a non-disabled woman would never have been allowed to remain single, childless and living away from home, but in my case they seem to have accepted that I am not going to follow the traditional route.

'Oh well. Perhaps it's a blessing in disguise. Kismet. Even an able-bodied woman can't keep a husband these days. So what chance for you?'

'Jo kujjh likhea hoea.' Whatever's written will be.

'You're getting much older now, bhenji,' my sister-in-law said recently.

'Yes, I had noticed unfortunately.'

'Well, you can't be alone for the rest of your life, everybody needs someone close to them. Besides, you need someone to help you now, so what about when you're an old lady?'

To my amazement, she suggested that, in the current absence of a partner, I should adopt a child.

'What?' I ask incredulously. 'You mean become a single parent?'

'Yes,' the family indignantly reply. 'That doesn't matter, it's not even important.'

How do I interpret this new line of thinking? It seems bizarre. Have they suddenly become open-minded, or is it just another hidden agenda? I notice that nothing is said about whether I want to have children or not; nothing about a child's right to childhood rather than caring for a parent. Actually the idea of adoption is really attractive to me, though not practical at this juncture of my life.

It's true that I'm getting older. True that I've taken a decisive hand in shaping my life. True that I've been shaped by events. Things I had no control over as well as those I could control. It has been a long and turbulent journey so far.

Whatever is written.

Not Exactly Eye to Eye

Michele Wates

In the middle of the night
it suddenly dawns
that my son must be
the same height as me –
'If I still have a height,
now that I sit down –
and I am pleased
to mark the moment
in my mind,
if not on the wall.

Next day he says,
'You can't come to parents' evening,'
and I draw myself up
to my seated height and say,
'I won't allow your prejudice to prevent me.'
Good and confrontational,
as an offensive teenager
and an affronted parent
are bound to be,
and we glare at each other;
not exactly eye to eye
but on the level.

Intervals

Sylvia Dick Gomez

Two in the morning. Gotta get up again; gotta go pee. Can't move. Can't move the legs *at all*. Can't hardly get the right arm out from under. Oh shit! Here we go again. The MS must be getting worse again. Desperately, I roll and haul myself to half-sitting, only to fall back, flat on my back, laughing: Kiki, 18 pounds of feline indifference, is curled over my lower legs. Draped carelessly above the dark calico fur is the long, tan arm of a ten-year-old girl. Her bare torso blocks my knees. Her feet are tucked under my arm. I hear the gentle snoring/purring of these two elegant creatures. Blissfully unaware, they have me totally immobilized.

Better not laugh; don't wanna pee. Struggling and grunting, I disturb them enough to perch precariously on the edge, before transferring to the chair. Roll in the dark. Transfer to the toilet. How many times have I made this trip? How many more are left before the MS also takes away this private little journey? Play the film backward; to the chair, to the bed. My sleeping companions squawk and stir restlessly at the sudden intrusion. They have kept the covers deliciously warm.

Awake. Thinking. Remembering. A good friend with multiple sclerosis was visiting the other week. She's a few years older than I; intellectually active, thoughtful, childless, with a similar level of disability. 'Wow! How do you manage?' she asked me. 'I can't imagine living with MS and having to take care of a child, too.'

I think I answered truthfully: 'I can't imagine living with MS and *not* having a child to take care of.'

*

Remembering. Marjorie was a year old when they diagnosed me. They told me not to count on returning to work. But I was going to be one of those people who would never have another attack, never get any worse. So I went back to work again, and again, and again, until I couldn't anymore.

'Have you started toilet training yet?' asked the other mothers in the play group. Were they kidding? It was all I could do to keep myself dry. Crouching together behind the bushes in the park, so thankful not to have to do it alone. She was about three when I began using a scooter, and she loved it.

'Come! Look!' she called out to the preschool teacher, 'What Mommy got me! So we can go faaasst!' Riding on the scooter together. Riding on the stairglide. Climbing into bed with Mommy to read stories. Mommy falls asleep first.

There were hard times, too, of course. Crawling down the hall dragging her by the rompers for a 'time-out'. Then sitting by the door weeping. Standing outside the restaurant, take-out in one hand and cane in the other. The kid is lying on the cement and screaming, 'Up! Up!!' Me, leaning against the storefront for support. Forgetting all the times I must have seen other parents in this predicament. What I wouldn't give to be able to lift her, to put her over my shoulder, to take her home. But you see, officer, I can't.

We got through all that; we got through the kindergarten that required me to crawl up a half-dozen steps; the hospitalization, when even though children weren't allowed in bed with patients, a kind nurse discreetly pulled the curtain; the Daddy who left the garbage bags blocking the exit door, his heavy tool box on the wheelchair, his heavy words on our memories. He hollered. Then he left.

'Your husband is more handicapped than you are,' observed the counsellor. By that time Big Sister had joined our family. Daddy's teenage daughter. Oh, how he raged when Karla chose to stay with me – me, the crazy, gimpy stepmother. We clung together, the three of us, survivors on a raft. But we didn't go down, did we, kids?

No, we moved to a new place with new people. A place which, though not perfect, was not as surprised at the sight of a disabled parent in the supermarket being assisted by her daughters. We formed new friendships, and cemented old ones. We grew.

Perhaps, I would have left my chair behind and gone kayaking on Sausalito Bay without Marjorie. Maybe, someone other than Karla would have insisted on pushing me into the Tuoleme River, dragging me out into the chilly mountain water buoyed along in her arms. It is easier to go out on Halloween dressed as an enormous pink butterfly when you have a small child to accompany you. After all, someone has to climb the steps to reach the doorbell.

No doubt, I could have found another algebra student to tutor. One who did not keep me up nights worrying where she was and with whom. Someone who would not break my heart, in order to be reassured that I loved her anyway. But, would this other person have allowed me to dry her tears with my shirt? Would she have written me a poem entitled 'Mom'?

Five in the morning, now. Another bathroom run. Returning to bed, I roust out both child and cat, take Marjorie's cold comforter from the floor, let her take my warm one. Two more hours till the alarm rings, and we get ready for school.

She's come a long way from the frightened seven-year-old who pulled me out of my chair with the strength of her anguish. Under my tutelage, she has learned to skate, to bike, to swim. She can read chapter books, and do her times tables up to 12. She sings in the chorus, and attends an endless round of birthday parties, excursions, and 'play dates'. She is happy, and she knows it.

There are advantages to having a disabled parent, in her

opinion. You can get lots of attention, if they don't go out to work. And you can cut the lines at Disneyland.

'I hate it!' she told me the other day, quite out of the blue. 'I hate it so much!'

'What do you hate?'

'MS. I hate it when it won't let you do things, when it makes you sad.'

For they have seen me very sad. They have seen me hang my head and weep in frustration, in fear, in anger, in pain. I try to shield them from the worst of it, but sometimes my grief just boils over. Most of my life I have been independent, future-oriented to a fault, focused outward. But now it seems my life must revolve around self-care, the next trip to the toilet. Like the Cheshire Cat in *Alice in Wonderland*, I am fading out bit by bit, and ultimately there is nothing to be done.

I fear dependency, loss of privacy, becoming a burden. I fear discomfort, physical and emotional. So much for the myth of the courageous crip! My mutual dependence with the children, however, is a source of strength, of insight: after all, who among us is truly independent?

Marjorie climbed on my lap, one horrible, terrible, no good day, careful as always to avoid the control box. Her long legs dangled over the sides of the chair, and she hugged me as we slowly circled together.

'I will help you, Mommy,' she assured me. 'We (a long list of family and friends) will all help you. We love you.'

Then she hopped off and announced, 'I'm hungry. Will you make me French toast? Three pieces? Please? May I have a friend over? When can we go to the movies? Let's sing a song!'

The song is on the radio. Time to get up. Both the legs are 'dancing' this morning. Don't forget your lunch. No, I don't remember where you left your shoes. Yes, I will read to you while you eat breakfast, but you have to hurry. At last, dressed and packed; fed and brushed; adequately hugged and kissed; she is ready. I am ordered to sit by the window and wave good-bye. Frantically, she bangs for me to open it, and when I do, gives me one last kiss.

'I'll miss you awfully!' she cries, and with a wave, skips off across the patio.

I start my morning routine. I can see it coming (Lord, don't let it be soon!), the day when I will need assistance with these simple tasks: other hands will bathe me, pull on the elastic stockings, steady the glass to take the medicine. Just have to live with it. Enjoy my solitude while I can.

After lunch. Better take a nap. Be rested when she comes home. As I pull up the covers, there is a whiff of sweet, childish sweat. When the cat comes back, I let her stay.

A Child of Both Countries

Corbett Joan O'Toole

I always knew that I wanted to be a mom. In my twenties I had cats. They helped me realize that I was not yet ready to parent children. When Jenny and I got together in our late twenties she was already a foster mother to two teenagers. So my mothering plans were put on hold for a while. In my thirties I tried a number of times to get pregnant but with no luck. By the time I was forty my life was great and there were no children on the horizon, so I began to accept that I was going to be childless.

Then a few months after my forty-second birthday, my friend Atsuko and I were at a meeting. During the break she turned to me and said, 'Corbett, would you like a baby?' Without hesitation I said, 'Yes.' And so began the adoption process and the odyssey that led Jenny and me to Meecha.

Jenny and I had long talks about having a child so late. Jenny had already raised a brood. She was ready to travel, to be unfettered by children's schedules. But I wanted to have a child. We agreed that I would be primary caregiver – the one to take Meecha to doctor's appointments, to meet with teachers, and so on; that if Meecha was sick, I would change my schedule to accommodate her.

When I went to pick up Meecha, I was only worried about one thing, 'Will she like new adventures as much as I do?' Everyone else in my life was worried about the practical things: How will you hold her and move her around? How will you accommodate both your disabilities? How will all your differences still allow you to parent effectively? But I was just wondering how we were going to get along. Would we enjoy the same things: playing in the water, traveling, meeting new people?

My daughter had lived in an adoption facility for her first ten months and I was concerned that she might be very fearful of new experiences. Within a few days, I knew that everything was going to be okay. We were staying in a hotel while processing paperwork. In the hotel lobby there was a small ramp. At first I came down the ramp very slowly with my daughter sitting in my lap, held on by my purse. But when she didn't complain, I began to increase my speed and soon she was laughing.

The next day, Jenny and I decided to give her a bath. There were no baby facilities, so we decided that I would get into the nice, deep tub. We filled it with slightly warm water and Jenny lifted Meecha in to me. As soon as Meecha's feet hit the water, she began to laugh and gurgle. She and I stayed in the water until all our digits puckered. Jenny and I said, 'Well, I guess she really is our kid – she loves the water like we do.' And in many ways, that was the end of all my worries.

If you ignore the facts that everyone in our family is disabled, that there are two mothers, that the adults and child are of different races – well, we seem like everyone else. I jokingly say that I belong in four completely different parenting groups: disabled parents; parents of disabled children; interracial families; lesbian parents. If I only had the time for all those support groups! Our set-up confounds many people. I have post-polio syndrome and use a wheelchair. Jenny looks non-disabled but has a serious back disability as well as diabetes. Most people assume from looking at Jenny that she would do all the lifting. It feels good to challenge assumptions. In October 1997 I organized, and Jenny filmed, an international conference on parents with disabilities. Lizzie Longshaw from Zimbabwe came and stayed with us until after Halloween. Here is the scene that greeted people as they opened their door to us: a small Asian girl in a bright green manual wheelchair; a mahogany-skinned African woman with one arm; a large white woman with sparkling blue eyes and an electric wheelchair to match;

and another white, apparently non-disabled, woman smiling at her family. And to us, it was wonderful.

I make plans that both accept and accommodate the realities of our lives. I sent Meecha to day-care at 18 months old. I figured that she needed lots of time with other children who wanted to play the same games as she did. I also acknowledged that it is physically impossible for me to care for her all the time. My body needs breaks from lifting her and caring for her. Also, as a disabled child, she needs lots of exposure to, and experience with, the non-disabled world.

It's been a very interesting experience, being a physically disabled adult with a physically disabled child. Most pre-school and day-care centers are not wheelchair accessible. Most have no experience with disabled children or parents. When Meecha was 15 months old, we went to a weekly parent and disabled child class. One day we came into the room and there were a number of new parents. They were shocked when I came rolling in with Meecha on my lap and I put her on the floor near some toys. When she told me that she wanted a toy that was a little farther away, I told her to get it herself. When one of the parents reached for it, I asked her to let Meecha do it. In answer to their surprised faces, I joked, 'You know, the really hard thing about having a disabled mother is that she makes her kid do everything for herself.'

When Meecha turned three years old, the local school district became responsible for her education. After much struggle, Meecha now goes to a fully integrated public pre-school.

Meecha spends her mornings in a class of disabled and non-disabled children where her teachers are trained in Special Education. Her afternoons are spent across the hall in an almost totally non-disabled class with regular education teachers. Her Special Education services will phase out within the next two years.

My disabled presence in the professional planning meetings at the school is vital. I come to the table as a full partner. All my knowledge about having a physical disability equals, or in many cases supersedes, the professionals' training and degrees. Most tellingly, they are usually offering 'help' as the solution for inaccessibility, whilst I am pushing for independent inclusion. I say to them, 'Your option makes her unnecessarily dependent on a non-disabled person. That is completely unrealistic except for the very rich. I am on a fixed income. Meecha needs to find ways to be independent in an inaccessible world. Her life and her future depend on it.'

Meecha is now five years old. She is a brilliant, wildly funny child who never fails to make me laugh. She is determined, clear-headed and totally wonderful. Strangers often remark that she is able to play by herself very well for a long time. Meecha's early months were spent in a small bed, lying on her back; she had to be self-entertaining to survive. When she came to me, I supported this trait. I am an older parent with limited mobility. I wanted a kid who could be in the same room with me and be playing on her own.

In some ways, it's been very important to me that Meecha expects to do things for herself. I know so many disabled adults who are not independent because their families protected them – never expected them to use a bathroom alone, for example. So with Meecha, I push her to expect to be independent and assist her as she needs it (and when she asks for it). It's in many ways based on my mother's parenting of me. She figured that she had a simple decision: train me to be part of the world, or keep me protected. I am very happy with her decision and I am passing it on to Meecha.

When Meecha and I first met, she did not speak nor did she understand English. So I borrowed from deaf sign language – and right from the first day I presented her with choices. I learned to hold up two toys and give her the one that she stared at. From the beginning, I have worked consciously to help Meecha see the world as providing lots of options. It is up to her to decide how to use them.

To me, far too often the world either tells disabled people that there are no options or makes a decision for us. I want Meecha to know that she always has choices – even if all the options are lousy ones! For example, she recently became toilet trained. Yet when we are going out, I tell her about the expected accessibility so that she can decide whether to wear panties and maybe depend on a stranger for help, or wear diapers. The choice is entirely hers. To some non-disabled parents this is heresy – they tell me that once she wears panties I should throw out the diapers. But our reality is different. I cannot help her use an inaccessible bathroom and she cannot use one by herself. But even without access, she has a choice of how to handle the situation. To me these are the kinds of choices she will have to make her entire life, so she can practice them now. Also, as an older mother I cannot guarantee that I will live to help her with her adulthood, so I need to teach her now about being smart.

One sign that Meecha believes she has options happened in Mexico. We were visiting Alicia Contreras in San Luis Potosi – a rural area. Alicia is organizing disabled people there and we were meeting with the Disabled Women's Independent Living Center (CEVIMUDI). One day, Alicia's friend Luz did not show up. Meecha was very concerned and asked Alicia about Luz's absence. Alicia stated that Luz's father did not allow her to go out if she would need to do her intermittent catheterization away from home. Meecha was dumbfounded. She made Alicia repeat the explanation many times and still did not accept it. To her it was inconceivable that bathroom issues would interfere with having fun.

I take Meecha with me nearly every time I travel. I figure that she's going to be part of the disabled adult community so she can be in it now. I also feel that whatever she learns on the road is as valuable as any classroom teaching. In all my work, Meecha is an active participant. She is often an important ambassador of change. In Mexico our presence as a mother and daughter in wheelchairs did more to show possibilities than any training I conducted. By traveling alone, we showed people the undeniable promise of a full and independent life. We also showed people that disabled children can be loved in their wholeness and proudly included.

What's been the easy part of being a disabled parent? Having a child to share adventures with, having a supportive spouse, laughing, seeing the world in a new way, opening non-disabled people's minds about who disabled people are and how we live, having other disabled parents to talk to.

What's been the hard part? The fact that my disability has gotten much worse from the constant physical strain, not being able to help my kid when she needs it, knowing that the world will hurt her for being disabled and being powerless to prevent that hurt, and not having the money to get help even when I needed it.

But whatever the difficulties, the disabled community has been the best source of ideas, support and solutions. Last year I was getting concerned that Meecha was not toilet trained. She was getting close to four years old and showed no interest. So I went to the community because I knew that that was where the answers were – not in some books, not with the doctors, but with the real professionals, women with cerebral palsy.

I live within the disability community – it houses my work and my life. It's a community in which many people have suffered greatly to have even the hint of an independent 'normal' life. We all know people who did not make it – who are institutionalized – who even died. So we look at life from a survivors' perspective; we know it can all be taken away if we are not diligent. We know that society does not want us to survive – selective abortions, the withholding of life-preserving medical treatment to disabled infants, physician-assisted suicide, health care restrictions, nursing homes. Many of us have fought so hard to survive that we did not get to have children.

I am part of the first generation that have been able to live our entire lives outside of institutions (no segregated education, hospital schools, nursing homes). Not all of us have had these choices but there are more of us than ever before. In order to stay alive and independent many of us have had to focus our working lives on defining the experience of disabled people and fighting for our basic rights. I hope that Meecha's generation can choose whatever career they want.

When Meecha comes into a room of disabled people they know she is their child; not just because they are her friends but because she so clearly represents their hope for immortality. They left home and blazed a trail in a new world. She is the second generation child who gets to remember the old ways – and learns from the new – a child of both countries.

So Meecha is treated like a precious commodity – a rare child who is growing up within the disabled community, someone who knows who we are and will remember our ways; whose everyday experience is validated and reflected back to her. Meecha is loved as we never were – she is seen in her wholeness. It's a priceless gift, for her and for us.

Bigger than the Sky

Adina Frieden

I am 15 years old, lying stomach down on my unmade bed. The pages of *The Baby Trap* are split open before me, and I am reading feverishly. I am captivated by the author's descriptions of jet-setting to Paris with her husband, their passionate sex life aided by her lithe and stretch mark free body, and her pursuit of sculpture, writing, and gourmet cooking. She explains that she is living her dream lifestyle because she's avoided the shackles of motherhood. I am completely swayed. I have no idea that in the future it will be my cystic fibrosis, rather than my own preferences, that impacts on my reproductive choices. But for now, I'm swooning in fantasies of childless bliss coupled with a gorgeous, millionaire husband.

I am 21 years old and I sit on a hard chair. Across from me, the spiky-haired intake worker asks in a curt, no-nonsense manner why I want to have a tubal ligation. She leans over the battered desk and tells me she is concerned because I'm only 21 and sterilization is a 'forever decision'. I answer that I have a genetic disease called cystic fibrosis, to which she responds, 'Never heard of it.' I try to explain a little about my constant cough, frequent lung infections and how I don't want to pollute the gene pool. She scrawls something on my chart and frowns. I don't think I should add that I want to have lots of sex with my new boyfriend and not worry about birth control. She tells me I really need to take time to process my feelings and recommends I return for another appointment. However, the next time I sit across from her, she's all smiles and support as she eagerly thrusts a bundle of papers at me to sign and scans the calendar for the earliest available surgery date. I suspect she may have had a chat with the clinic doctor who knows all about cystic fibrosis and vigorously agrees with my decision to be sterilized.

A week later I lie in a hospital bed inside the Women's Choice Clinic in Berkeley, waiting for my operation. All I remember is feeling a little prick in my arm and dropping off into a dream in which I hear voices exclaiming, 'You're doing great, nice and easy, good job!' When I awake I am back in the same bed, wondering when they will wheel me in for surgery. A clinic nurse comes to check on me and I ask how much longer it will be. She laughs and tells me, 'Honey, it's over, you're all finished!'

I spend the afternoon recovering at my friend's apartment, lying on his sofa and cramping. Once in a while, I feel this weird kind of sadness but I dismiss it, thinking I am just wiped out from the surgery. The tubal ligation is what I wanted and since cystic fibrosis is life-shortening anyway, not having the option to become pregnant and have a child feels like the least of my worries. I sip herb tea, grimace, and pray that my pain goes away soon.

I am 28 years old and six women are sprawled around my living room in Albuquerque, New Mexico. We are having our weekly class in Re-Evaluation Counseling, a process that helps release painful, deep-seated emotional hurts. We also have discussions about some of the sources of our pain and tonight's topic is Women's Self-Image. Our teacher throws out the question, 'What comes up for you when you think about how you see yourself as a woman?'

Mary Sue, who is very pregnant with her first child, goes first. She fumbles, blushes, but then starts talking about how she never felt like she fit the definition of a woman until she became pregnant. I cannot stop staring. Her cherubic cheeks, her fleshy wrists, her light pink maternity jumpsuit; all bursting with about-to-be-mama energy.

I'm startled out of my daze by my teacher's voice, 'Okay, Adina, your turn, what would you like to share?' 'Uh, um,' I begin, but before I can even form one cogent sentence, I start sobbing non-stop, and it's like being pulled under by river rapids of grief. Minutes later, I finally raise up my head and I feel pummeled and bruised by what I thought never existed. My longing to be a mother. And the knowing, like a sinkhole, that I will never get to be one.

I am 33 years old and he is five years old and my arms are open wide. We are lying side by side in my little patch of yard and I am showing him the answer to my question, 'Know how much I love you?' He giggles and asks how much, how much? 'Bigger than the sky!' I shout and then I dive bomb him an embrace and boom! We're one big explosion of joy.

His name is Justin. He came into my life three years ago, about the same time I moved back to Berkeley to start an internship at the Center for Independent Living. The Center has helped me change the way I perceive my cystic fibrosis; from an illness that bears much shame and inadequacy to a disability that challenges and ultimately empowers. Another big help has been my boyfriend Phil, a high-level quadraplegic and long-time CIL staffer, who provides answers to everything I've ever wanted to know, especially to that intriguing sex and disability question!

Soon after Phil and I fell in love, I got to know his best friend Mark, the father of Justin. Several months later, Justin's mom drifted off into an alcoholic haze and Mark got full custody. Significantly stressed and overwhelmed as a single parent, Mark was thrilled when I offered to hang out with his kid. Now, a lot of my life is on 'Justin time'. Bike rides, park swings, Saturday tumbling class, weekly sleep-overs, taking him to exotic lands including Adventure, Fairy, and Disney.

It's also about holding him close when he's crying about the bully in preschool that calls him stupid-head, making up bed-time stories featuring a penguin named Ping-Pong, patiently teaching him shoe tying for the fiftieth time, and excitedly showing him the note that 'Santa Claus' left, ho-ho-ho-ing thanks for the pickle and 7-up.

He's confused about why his own mother, who has been on a drinking binge in Mexico for the past year, is never around. One night as I was tucking him into bed he asked, 'Well, you could be my mom, couldn't you?' I took a deep breath, drew him close to me and said, 'No, I am not your mother, but I love you very, very much and will always be here for you.' I try not to think that because my cystic fibrosis is progressive, 'always' is a loaded concept. Instead, I gaze into his cocoa-rich eyes, dancing with delight, and try just to be right here for him, right now.

'How much do I love you?' I repeat, feeling the grass tickling underneath us. This time he throws his arms around my neck and shouts in my ear, 'I know, I know, bigger than the sky!'

I am 41 years old and he is 13 and I decide to tell him, over bowls of rocky-road ice-cream, that I am dying. It has been three months since I contracted congestive heart failure and have had to use oxygen around the clock. I might have a year, maybe two, to live. I care less about the estimates and more about having to look into Justin's face and say, 'I may not live to see you graduate from high school.' After one of my friends shakes me up by pointing out how devastated Justin will be if I die and he is totally unprepared, I know I can't put it off any longer. We sit in my office that is also Justin's bedroom when he sleeps over, and I shut the door for privacy. Phil, who is now my husband, has offered to be with me when I tell Justin, but I know this is something that I need to do on my own.

I am so nervous I toss out a misguided, 'Justin, there's something I have to tell you, but it might upset you, so maybe I should wait until the morning.' He sighs and asks me a long drawn out wha-a-at, in that half annoyed, sullen tone puberty has blessed him with. I freeze up and detour by asking him how he sees my cystic fibrosis doing at this point. He just shrugs and says that the oxygen is a good thing because it's helping me, right?

I've forgotten how casual he can be around my disability. It's probably because I've never hidden any of my medical care from him. If anything, it became just another activity to engage us. He'd sit on my lap and I'd have him count how many smoke rings I could blow out of my nebulizer. Or as he got older, I'd let him whack the bottom of syringe holders on the tabletop before I set myself up for an antibiotic infusion. My constant coughing became like a background of white noise suffusing our time together. I even used oxygen at the high altitude Family Camp we had been going to for the past five summers.

It's so tempting to ride alongside his denial with a 'Hey dude, don't worry, I'm fine, I'll just have to wear this darn oxygen for the next thirty years.' Telling the truth feels like falling into a black hole but I tell myself I'm doing the right thing as I form the words.

'Justin, I'm at end-stage which means I could live between six months and several more years. And I want you to know that the worst part about dying, more than anything else, is having to leave you.'

Tears are rolling down his cheeks as I talk, and then he sobs for a long time. I feel numb, horrified at what I've done. At last he murmurs, 'This is probably the hardest thing I've ever had to deal with.' I whisper back, 'Me too.' We continue our talk in soft voices, him telling me he'd rather know the truth than be protected like a little kid, me telling him how the eleven years we've been together have been the best, the absolute best. Wiping away my own tears I say, 'But, you know, we'll go through all of this together, right?' He slowly nods his head and then I reach out to grasp his strong brown fingers, amazed at how much his hand now outsizes my own.

I am 42 years old and he is 14 years old and we stand together in the darkness, oohing and ahhing at the silvery blur of Comet Hale-Bopp. We have driven away from city lights and up to Inspiration Point where we can savor its once-in-every-four-hundred-year appearance.

'Look Adina, over there!' With a sweep of his arm, Justin confidently locates and points out to me Polaris, Orion, and the Seven Sisters. I nod and smile, remembering the special award he got at Family Camp for setting up telescopes and assisting the visiting astronomer – 'Can you believe that's her name?' – Celeste.

It's been about a year since our initial discussion about my death. I am still at end-stage, but life has blessedly continued. With my portable oxygen in tow, I have attended Family Orientation Night at his prospective high school, and had a front row seat at the school play when he headed up the Tech Crew. We even took a weekend 'Funship Cruise' to Ensenada but spent both evenings watching videos in our stateroom, rather than having to endure 'Broadway at Sea' in the Americana Lounge or be met by the sotted, over-friendly greetings of fellow passengers. Each time we reminisce about the trip we usually chant 'Hated it' and burst out laughing. Every Tuesday night I drive him to his archery league where he is the youngest member and racks up increasingly impressive scores.

I've also lived to experience more door slammings, frequent snarls of 'leave me alone,' headache-producing soliloquies of exactly why he's right and I'm wrong, and the infamous 'There's nothing else to do' mantra whenever I tell him he's spending too much time playing computer games. It's a drag. However, when I realize I'm still HERE to witness all these hairpin turns of his adolescence, the less than charming behavior becomes much easier to deal with.

'What's that?' Justin gasps, breaking my reverie and clutching on to my arm as ghostly sounding howls pierce through the darkness.

'Wow! Coyotes,' I whisper and I can feel his body tighten a little in fear.

'Don't worry, honey,' I add, calmly. 'See they're way out in that canyon, far away from us. We're perfectly safe here,' and he lets out a loud whoosh of relief. We continue to stand by the railing and he begins to twist strands of my hair around his fingers, a habit from childhood and, I suspect, a way of still making physical contact now that he's way too cool to ask for hugs or cuddles.

Looking up into the night sky, I think about how my experiences with Justin are like a unique constellation of parenthood; different from others, but still just as amazing. I realize I attained these experiences because I learned to move past limiting images of both parenthood and disability. I am so grateful I did as I now stand with my boy, watching a once in a lifetime comet dazzle above us.

Contributors' Notes

Philippa Armstrong lives in Devon. She is a freelance consultant and a mature student. Thinking in pictures, she can find words alien and believes intuition is underrated. She likes shopping, chocolates, cuddles, teenagers sometimes, and border collies always. She is fiercely proud, advocating disability arts in preference to genetic engineering.

Ellen Basani grew up in South Australia in the 1950s and trained as a social worker. Since 1980 she has lived in England. She has trained as a voice therapist, assisting people to liberate their vocal uniqueness, as she feels she has finally been able to liberate her own. She enjoys exploring, and sharing through training and after-dinner speaking, the fascinating journey from denial through to celebration of disability.

Heather Beattie, her husband David and son Connor live in County Down, Northern Ireland. Heather has Lupus, a spinal instability, and a fractured spine. Much of her life is currently seen through the haze created by the morphine she takes to control pain. Until recently she worked as an accredited counsellor in private practice.

Rosangela Berman Bieler is a Brazilian journalist, publisher and disability rights advocate, currently living in the Washington DC area of the USA. Founder of the independent living movement in Brazil, she is also the founder and current director of the Inter-American Institute on Disability. Rosangela has been a quadriplegic since an automobile accident in 1976, and uses a wheelchair. She is married to Michael, and their daughter Mel is now a teenager.

Catherine Bradbury lives in Oxford and has two grown-up daughters. She has always been interested in poetry and has just completed the first term of an evening class entitled 'The Practise of Poetry', which she thoroughly enjoyed and hopes will help her to improve her writing.

Frances Brown lives in a town in the south west of Cornwall. The sea is about three miles away and there are four lovely beaches. She likes swimming, using the computer, cooking, walking and word-search puzzles. She also enjoys music, watching TV and being with her son.

Karen Peterson Butterworth lives with her husband Brian in the New Zealand village of Otaki, near Wellington, where she writes and grows food for home use. Her book *Mind Over Muscle: Surviving Polio in New Zealand* (Dunmore Press, 1994), is still in print and she has had journalistic articles, fiction and poetry published in New Zealand, Australia, Canada and the USA.

Shallo Chand grew up amongst cotton fields in sunshine yellow India. Brilliant white snow covered England when, in December 1965, she arrived with her parents in search of a medical cure. Her childhood involved long-term hospital stays and dreaded special schools. Her real life began when she started work. Being a small cog in a huge wheel, however, left Shallo disillusioned and unfulfilled, so she is now studying for an MSc at Oxford University.

Alicia Contreras was born in 1966 in Mexico City. In 1992 she participated in a leadership program for disabled people and has become a strong fighter in the disability movement. In 1996 she started CEVIMUDI, an independent living centre for disabled women in San Luis Potosi. She is currently employed by the municipal government, working on a range of programs involving disabled people. Alicia Contreras loves meeting people from all over the world and has organized three US-Mexico exchange programs with Mobility International USA.

Merry Cross has, in her time, helped to found the disability movement in England; lived, loved and worked in Kenya; and acted with Graeae theatre company. She is now a freelance trainer and consultant on protecting disabled children from abuse. Her latest book, published by The Women's Press in 1998, is *Proud Child, Safer Child: A Handbook for Parents and Carers of Disabled Children*.

Liz Crow is a disabled writer, consultant and campaigner who has been active in the disabled people's movement for nearly two decades. Her work includes a range of social and political, travel and autobiographically-based pieces, as well as practical handbooks. Her writing has been published by The Women's Press, Disability Press and Rough Guide, as well as in various journals.

Jill Daly spent her late teens and most of her twenties working in a variety of European countries. On returning to England, she became a mature student and studied languages at university. After graduating, Jill became disabled, started working as a teacher and then moved into Equal Opportunities, working for a city council. She is now living in Nottingham, England, working as a full-time mum to two small boys, and is embarking on a new career as a writer.

Vicky D'aoust and her adoptive daughter Marianne live in Canada. Marianne currently goes to a residential school for the deaf. She wins medals for running and jumping in track and field and loves dancing. Vicky is a researcher, writer, advocate and devoted *X-Files* fan. She spends time crocheting, quilting and creating political works in the hope of changing the status quo.

Sue Firth is a Yorkshirewoman and as such calls a spade 'a bloody shovel'. Mike, the kindest man on God's earth, has steadfastly remained married to her for 25 years and they have two sons – Jim (15) and Tom (11). Before becoming ill Sue had hoped to train as an Anglican priest. Now she supports and counsels individuals with myalgic encephalo-myelitis (ME) and campaigns for greater recognition and awareness of how severe a disease this can be.

Adina Frieden was born on 21 September 1954 in Los Angeles, California, where she was raised. She earned degrees in psychology and counseling and worked as a counselor and Disability Rights advocate at the Center for Independent Living in Berkeley, California. There she met her husband, Phil. In the last two years of her life, Adina became a writer. After living almost 44 years with cystic fibrosis, Adina orchestrated her conscious death, surrounded by loved ones, on 21 June 1998. She was a self-proclaimed 'True Life Babe'.

Linda M Gordon experienced symptoms of her mental illness while a preschooler. She writes and speaks internationally about her experiences with panic disorder and manic depression as well as about the needs and abilities of parents with mental illness and the barriers they face. Linda worked for 25 years as a manager in software and applications design for large computer manufacturers. A single parent since 1986, she lives in Massachusetts, USA, with her two teenage sons.

Sylvia Dick Gomez lives in Northern California with her mother, younger daughter, Kiki the cat and a service dog named Miel. She considers herself a good mother-in-law, a fun-loving joker and a staunch supporter of the international working class.

Constance Hambwalula is 38 and lives in Zambia. As a child she had polio and became paralysed in one leg. She completed secondary education and trained in electronics but because of people's negative attitudes towards disability she could not find employment. Eventually she became an instructor in tailoring, cutting and design at a training college for disabled people and rose to the position of Principal. She currently works as an executive director for Zambia National Association of the Physically Handicapped.

Wendy S Harbour is late-deafened and is actively involved with the Deaf, disability, and gay and lesbian communities. She is a disability specialist at the University of Minnesota in the United States. Wendy is happy to leave parenting of children up to others right now, but she is a proud aunt and loving every minute of it. She and her partner reside in Minneapolis.

Laura Hershey is a poet, writer, activist, organizer, and consultant who lives in Denver, Colorado, USA. She and her partner, Robin Stephens, are former foster parents and hopeful future adoptive parents. Laura has spinal muscular atrophy and uses a power wheelchair, a voice-activated computer, daily attendant services and other supports to live independently and work creatively. More of Laura's poems and other writings are available on the Internet at: http://ourworld.compuserve.com/homepages/LauraHershey

Jodi Hoar lives in a loft apartment in downtown Toronto, Canada, with her partner, two of her three children, a roommate, two dogs and three cats. Besides trying to keep her head above the obvious chaos of living with that many 'beings', she is currently finishing a Master's degree in theology at the University of Toronto, where she is intersecting Queer Theory and Christianity.

Denise Sherer Jacobson spent 27 years trying to get out of the Bronx, New York, and finally succeeded in 1978. She now lives in a small house in the San Francisco Bay Area with husband Neil and teenage son David. The family hopes that the publication of Denise's first book, *The Question of David: A Disabled Mother's Journey Through Adoption, Family, and Life*, will bring fame, fortune and a bigger house!

Deborah Kent earns her living as a writer of children's books, both young-adult novels and non-fiction for younger readers. She worked in New York City as a psychiatric social worker but, before burnout could set in, she moved to San Miguel de Allende, a town in Mexico where many writers and artists have settled. It was there that she wrote her first book. She now lives in Chicago with her husband, children's-book author R Conrad (Dick) Stein, and their daughter Janna.

Jo Litwinowicz loves reading books about the old days and likes watching TV. She grew up in the south of England and spent much of her childhood in hospital. When at home she attended a school run by the Spastics Society which involved a daily round trip of nearly three hours. After studying shorthand, typing and English at residential college she worked in a sheltered workshop. Once married, Jo was more and more able to take control of her own life. She's still enjoying doing things her own way.

Chava Willig Levy is a New York-based lecturer, author, storyteller and singer. Her articles have appeared in magazines including *McCall's, Parents, Woman's Day* and *Family Circle*. Chava's lectures and workshops, some available on audiocassette, have earned her an international following. A vocalist whose repertoire embraces six languages, she is recording an album, *Half-Full to Overflowing*, which celebrates uncommon lives. An Internet enthusiast, Chava's e-mail address is primerib@idt.net.

Micheline Mason is a survivor of segregated residential

education, and has been involved in disability politics all her adult life. She is a writer, campaigner, single parent, ally and has taken a leading role in the campaign for Inclusive Education in Britain. Micheline works as a Disability Equality Trainer and consultant and has produced many invaluable resources, including 'Disability Equality in the Classroom' available from the Alliance for Inclusive Education.

Jenni Meredith, performance poet, columnist, computer artist and community arts worker, has lived for the last 20 years on the Isle of Wight. She has been known to do gigs with her son, Eddie, a clown and children's entertainer. Her writing, often reflecting personal experience of disability, has been published in magazines and anthologies, broadcast on radio, and performed at readings in Italy as well as throughout England. She won an award for her animated poetry pop video, 'Through The Pane', and is currently working on an interactive CD.

Sue Napolitano was lucky enough to miss the Second World War but be in time for the sixties, the women's liberation movement and the disabled people's movement. She became a parent in 1990 and this opened up new worlds of love, play and delight, as well as heaping on extra dollops of oppression. Having survived polio at the age of seven, Sue spent the next 40 years making her mark on the world. She finally succumbed to cancer and died in 1996.

Sue Norris lives in North West England and is very proudly 50 years old. She enjoys philosophy and architecture, and describes herself as a people-watcher. She usually writes around 50 poems each day and, at the last count, had created over 21,000 complete poems. Sue is currently unable to go out and is facing many difficulties but, if she had a million pounds, one of the first things she would do is sail around the world in a ship.

Rhoda J Olkin lives in Northern California with her husband and two children. 'Banality' is part of a quintet of disability stories she has written. In addition to her fiction she has also written a non-fiction book for therapists treating families with disabilities (*Disability-Affirmative Therapy*, Guildford, 1999). She is a polio survivor and a professor of psychology.

Corbett Joan O'Toole is a disabled woman, mother, activist and videomaker. She is the Director of the Disabled Women's Alliance (USA) and gives workshops internationally on women and disability. Late in life she became a mother for the first time and it's better than she could ever have imagined. She is making films so that her disabled daughter will know about all the wonderful disabled women throughout the world.

Janet Pedley lives on the edge of a big city in the north of England. She likes to go out every day to meet her friends and twice a week she attends a day centre for people with learning-difficulties. Most of all, Janet enjoys her weekends when she goes to visit her family and can spend time with her mum, her sisters and her young son.

Alana Theriault lives in Berkeley, California. She works, makes art and food, listens to loud music, and enjoys her friends and family. She writes poetry, letters and essays exploring disability, self-image and sexuality. Alana has no children and enjoys the children growing up around her.

Julia Dolphin Trahan is a poet, videographer, essayist and theatrical performer. She became disabled at the age of eleven following a car accident. Before moving to Hawaii she lived in the Bay Area of California and worked for six years in the heart of the gay and disability cultures. Julia Dolphin Trahan lists the following amongst her hobbies: writing autobiographical narrative, weight lifting, going out to breakfast, drinking coffee, talking, playing on computer, sex, swimming, arm-crank cycling and performing on stage. To view her writings check: http://members.tripod.com/Dolphin J/Antonina.html

Beth Weil had a cerebral hemorrhage at the age of 39 while performing *Bluegrass* on stage in Southern California. She is now disabled and has brain damage. However, none of this interferes with her ability to work, and she has resumed her job as a graphic artist for Arhoolie Records in El Cerrito, California. She is divorced and at the time of writing has joint custody of her two children, Matt and Rachel Diamant.

Resources

Organisations/Internet addresses

Alliance for Inclusive Education Campaigns to end compulsory segregation in education throughout the UK. Unit 2, 70 South Lambeth Road, London SW8 IRL Tel: 0171 735 5277. E-mail: ALLFIE@btinternet.com

Cal-WILD (California – Women's International Linkage on Disability) is a free international e-mail list service open only to women with disabilities and women allies. Over 170 women from more than 20 countries exchange experiences, information and ideas on issues related to women with disabilities. To subscribe send an e-mail message to: owner-cal-wild@igc.org

Diana Michelle's Home Page An Internet-based resource for parents with disabilities. Information on adaptive parenting equipment and a listing of organisations, publications, and relevant articles on parenting with a disability. Also includes information on adoption and reproductive options for potential parents with disabilities. Includes the Parent Empowerment Network, a worldwide, e-mail information and support group for parents with disabilities and their partners.
http://ourworld.compuserve.com/homepages/TrishandJohn
Contact: Trish Day, Project Director, Diana Michelle's Home Page
E-mail: 74731.2325@compuserve.com
Tel: 301 464 9484 (USA)

DPPi (Disability, Pregnancy & Parenthood International) runs an information service for disabled parents and professionals in the UK and publishes a quarterly international journal.

DPPi can be contacted at: 45 Beech Street, London EC2P 2LX Tel: 0171 628 2811 Fax: 0171 628 2833 Textphone: 0171 256 8899. E-mail: dppi@eotw.co.uk

Website: freespace.virgin.net/disabled.parents

ParentAbility, a UK wide peer support network of disabled parents, **Parents Too**, a campaigning consortium, & **DDPi** are, at the time of publication, proposing to form a single UK wide organisation which will undertake peer support, information services and campaigning within the UK and also liaise with initiatives in other countries. Contact this new organisation via DPPi.

Right From the Start, a Maternity Alliance project for parents with learning difficulties, held a conference in September 1998 in conjunction with Kent and Canterbury Hospital Trust to examine gaps in maternity service provision, which disadvantage women with learning difficulties. A report on some of the work that was presented is available from the Maternity Alliance: 45 Beech Street, London EC2P 2LX Tel: 0171 588 8583.

E-mail: ma@maternity-all.demon.co.uk

The Special Parenting Service has developed a range of resources, including videos, parenting skill cards, and an assessment manual for professionals supporting parents with disabilities.

Further details from: Sue McGaw, Head of Special Parenting Service, Trecare NHS Trust, Walsingham Place, Truro, Cornwall TR1 2RP Tel: 01872 263334 Fax: 01872 263686.

Through the Looking Glass is a community non-profit organisation, based in California, which emerged from the disability independent living movement in 1982. TLG's mission has been to create, demonstrate and encourage resources and model early intervention services

which are non-pathological and empowering.
2198 Sixth Street, Suite 100, Berkeley CA 94710-2204, USA
Tel (voice): 800 644 2666 TDD/TTY: 800 804 1616
Local: 510 848 1112 Fax: 510 848 4445
E-mail: TLG@lookingglass.org Website:
http://www.lookingglass.org

Publications

Disability, Pregnancy & Parenthood international. A forum for professionals and parents to exchange information and experience – quarterly journal produced by DPPi.

Linda Toms Barker, Megan Kirschbaum et al, *You May Be Able to Adopt: A Guide to the Adoption Option for Prospective Mothers with Disabilities and their Partners*, Through the Looking Glass, Berkeley, 1997.

Linda Toms Barker and Vida Maralani, *Challenges and Strategies of Disabled Parents: Findings from a National Needs Survey of Parents with Disabilities*, Berkeley Planning Associates for Through the Looking Glass, Berkeley, 1998.

Mukti Jain Campion, *Who's Fit to be a Parent?*, Routledge, London, 1995. A critical examination of the processes and criteria employed by professionals in assessing fitness to parent.

Anita DeMoss, Judith Rogers et al, *Adaptive Parenting Equipment*, Through the Looking Glass, Berkeley, 1995.

Anne Finger, *Past Due: A Story of Disability, Pregnancy and Birth*, The Women's Press, London, 1991; Seal Press, Seattle, 1990. A thought-provoking account of the author's experience and exploration of reproductive rights, disability, pregnancy and childbirth.

Denise Sherer Jacobson, *The Question of David: A Disabled Mother's Journey Through Adoption, Family and Life*, Creative Arts Book Company, Berkeley, 1999. Hardcover ISBN 0 88739 145 1, paperback ISBN 0 88739 201 6.Order from CAB: 833 Bancroft Way, Berkeley CA 94710, USA Tel: 800 848 7789.

Veronica Lewis, *A Good Sign Goes a Long Way*, RNID and the Maternity Alliance. Research into the experiences and needs of deaf women during pregnancy, birth and beyond. Booklet out of print, photocopy available from the Maternity Alliance.

Jenny Morris (ed), *Encounters with Strangers: Feminism and Disability*, The Women's Press, London, 1996.

Judith Rogers, *Mother to Be: A Guide to Pregnancy and Birth for Women with Disabilities*, Demos Press. Currently updating – details from Through the Looking Glass.

Michele Wates, *Disabled Parents: Dispelling the Myths*, Radcliffe Medical Press in collaboration with the National Childbirth Trust, 1997. ISBN 1 85775 257 0.
RMP Tel: 01235 528820.
E-mail medical@radpress.win-uk.net
NCT publishing Tel: 01223 352790 Fax: 01223 460718
E-mail bpc@bpccam.demon.co.uk